College Scholarships for High School Students (grades 9-12)

Michael J. Neuwirth

This book does not contain comprehensive descriptions of scholarships or identify every available scholarship. It is intended as a general guide to help expedite the scholarship search process for high school students. References to websites and website addresses are provided for informational purposes only and do not constitute an endorsement of those websites. Website addresses are subject to change, expire, or be redirected without notice. While every effort has been made to make the content of this book accurate and current as of the publication date, the ultimate source for accurate, current and comprehensive content is the scholarship provider.

Editor: Jeanne E. Ross-Neuwirth

Higher Education Publishing

Dedication

To my children who never cease to amaze me. They are my inspiration!

To my wife for editing the book.

To all the students and families who pursue college scholarships. I wish you much success in your endeavor and beyond.

Table of Contents

CHAPTER ONE

Introduction & How to Use This Book

Welcome! If you have started searching for college scholarships, you are likely frustrated from countless hours of reading about scholarships that you ultimately are not eligible for. I shared your frustration. If you are new to the world of searching for college scholarships, I am pleased that you found this book before getting too involved in the process.

Before we begin, I would like to share my experience which ultimately led me to write this book. As a parent, I wanted to take the "search" burden off my children in order for them to concentrate on what I thought would be the more difficult part; the application process. I never imagined that finding college scholarships for which high school students are eligible to apply would become a full-time job!

Like most students and parents, I used standard research methods, such as books, the internet and scholarship search engines. These and other methods were all useful, but after spending over 1,000 hours, I can sum up my experience in two words: information overload! There were just too many scholarships to sort through and most were intended for students already enrolled in college. In some cases, I did not discover that high school students were ineligible to apply until I accessed the scholarship provider website for additional information. It became apparent that searching for college scholarships is a time consuming and frustrating experience for all high school students and their parents.

As the title states, this book focuses on college scholarships for which high school students in grades 9-12 are eligible to apply. It includes contests that provide awards for college tuition and other expenses. My goal is to prevent students from becoming discouraged and overwhelmed during the search process and potentially giving up before they even apply for scholarships. This book will make your research time more efficient and eliminate much of the frustration that comes with it.

Applying for college scholarships is important for several reasons. There is a financial benefit, an academic benefit and winning a scholarship can potentially improve your college admission prospects.

The financial reason is obvious. According to the College Board, the average cost of tuition and fees for a public college or university in 2015/2016 is $9,410 for state residents and $23,893 for out-of-state residents. The average cost of tuition and fees for a private college or university during this same period is $32,405. When you consider that room and board and other expenses at both public and private colleges and universities can be an additional $10,000-$15,000, it is no surprise that most students and their families experience "sticker shock" when they first receive their college financial aid (need-based and merit-based) package.

The academic reason is also important. Many scholarships require an essay and a demonstration of analytical thought and knowledge. Students will gain valuable research, writing and analytical experience that can be applied in college and beyond.

The third, and equally important, reason is to improve your college admission prospects. Winning a scholarship looks good on a college application regardless of the monetary award.

So how does this book assist you in searching for scholarships? Each scholarship is summarized and contains specific identifiers. By scanning through the identifiers, you can typically make a quick decision about whether to eliminate or consider that scholarship before reading through the entire summary. For example, if a scholarship is listed as applicable for high school seniors, you will move on to the next scholarship if you are a high school sophomore. If a scholarship is listed as requiring a minimum grade point average, you will move on to the next scholarship if you do not have that minimum grade point average. The scholarships are also organized by specific categories, such as merit-based, financial need-based, and degree and career interest, in order to further reduce the search time.

Before you begin evaluating scholarships, it is important to understand how we defined the following terms:

The term "**scholarship**" includes contests that provide awards for college tuition and other expenses.

For the purpose of this book, the term "**college**" includes universities.

Eligible Applicant refers to the high school grade level(s) that are eligible to apply for the scholarship. For example, a scholarship having *Eligible Applicant: Grades 9-10* means that high school freshmen and sophomores are eligible to apply, but high school juniors and seniors are not eligible to apply for the scholarship.

Some of the scholarships are also open to middle school or college students. For example, some of the essay, video and poetry contests. However, this book is intended for high school students and thus only identifies the eligible high school grade level(s).

Other Eligibility refers to other criteria that must be met in order to apply for the scholarship. For example, a specific citizenship, financial need, a minimum grade point average, state residency, certain affiliations and a specific type of college that the student must enroll at to receive the award.

GPA refers to the minimum high school grade point average required to apply for the scholarship.

Deadline refers to the scholarship application deadline as of the publication of this book. Most scholarships are listed with the deadline month. These scholarships are expected to use the same month in future years. Some scholarships are listed with a specific date.

If the deadline passed, students should refer to the provider website for its next deadline. If the provider website lists the scholarship as being "closed", do not assume that the scholarship has been terminated. This typically means that the scholarship application deadline for that period or year has expired. Students should return to the website at a later date for the next application cycle and deadline.

Financial Need refers to a "financial" component as one of the eligibility criteria for the scholarship. There is no standard formula to calculate or determine financial need. Scholarships may define financial need as meeting the eligibility for a Federal Pell Grant, having household income up to a specific maximum amount, or demonstrating financial hardship regardless of household income. The book includes the financial need definition when it was clearly defined on the scholarship provider's website.

Merit-Based refers to scholarships that are awarded based on a student's skill, ability or achievements without consideration for household income or financial hardship. For example, applicants may be evaluated on academics, leadership, community service, essay writing skills, artistic skill or entrepreneurship potential.

Awards are identified as "**renewable annually**" when students are required to reapply each year to continue receiving the awards. The book lists both the first year dollar amount award and the total dollar amount award over the course of the scholarship term. Students should understand that renewable scholarships typically have college academic and enrollment requirements for those awards to be renewed. For example, students may be required to maintain a specific minimum GPA while in college to continue receiving the scholarship. Students who win a renewable scholarship will receive the renewable requirements from the provider.

It is important to note that the scholarship summaries are based on a review of the rules, requirements, awards and deadlines that are posted on the scholarship provider website. In some cases, the provider was contacted directly for clarification. Every effort was made to ensure current information and to list scholarships that are projected to remain available well beyond the publication of this book. However, it is possible that some providers may change, restructure or end their scholarship program. For example, a provider that relies on a sponsor may need to revise or end the scholarship if the sponsor does not continue to participate in the program. Thus, the best source for current information will always be the provider website.

Lastly, I recommend that you use an Excel spreadsheet or equivalent method to record scholarships for which you are considering applying. For example, as you read through the scholarship summaries, you could record the name and provider of the scholarship, key eligibility requirements, such as GPA, the application deadline, the website address and the page number in this book where the scholarship is listed for future reference. This spreadsheet could then be used to track scholarships that you ultimately apply for.

CHAPTER TWO

National Scholarships/ Merit-Based

This chapter identifies national scholarships that are based solely on merit. For example, these scholarships may be awarded for high academic achievement, such as a high GPA or ACT/SAT score, participation in extra-curricular activities, elected leadership positions, volunteering for community service, or for an exceptional essay, video, poem, artistic or research submission.

The scholarships are listed in alphabetical order by scholarship name.

Appreneur Scholar Award

ELIGIBLE APPLICANT: Grades 9-12

OTHER ELIGIBILITY: Students anywhere in the world.

OVERVIEW: An annual technology contest for students to develop a working application. Students can enter their application as individuals or teams. The application must run on any of the current mobile application devices including iOS, Android, Windows, as well as smartwatches, wrist wear, Google Glass and other emerging platforms. The public will have an opportunity to vote on their favorite application, but a panel of judges will ultimately determine the winners. The applications will be judged on impact, scalability, originality, user interface and retention.

AWARD: $5,000 for two winners.

DEADLINE: November

PROVIDER: Living in Digital Times & Kay Family Foundation

WEBSITE: www.appreneurscholars.com

American College Foundation Visionary Scholarship

ELIGIBLE APPLICANT: Grades 9-12

OTHER ELIGIBILITY: U.S. citizen or legal resident.

OVERVIEW: A program to help students pay for college. Students register to receive their application package. The application process includes an essay (500 words) on the question "Why College is Important to Me?" Judges will select winners based on ability to follow guidelines and the essay.

AWARD: $1,000 to $5,000. The number of awards varies.

DEADLINE: April

PROVIDER: American College Foundation

WEBSITE: www.americancollegefoundation.org/college_ planning

American Foreign Services Association National High School Essay Contest

ELIGIBLE APPLICANT: Grades 9-12

OTHER ELIGIBILITY: U.S. citizen attending school in the U.S., its territories or overseas whose parents are not members of AFSA.

OVERVIEW: An annual essay (1,000-1,200 words) contest to encourage students to think and write about building peace through diplomacy. Students write from the perspective of a member of the U.S. Foreign Service assigned to one of eight bureaus within the Department of State or the U.S. Agency for International Development. The 2016 essay prompt asks students to write about peacebuilding solutions to a particular conflict or crisis that threatens U.S. interests abroad.

AWARD: The winner receives $2,500, a meeting with the Secretary of State and a fully-paid voyage with Semester at Sea. The runner-up receives $1,250 and a full scholarship to participate in the International Diplomacy Program of the National Student Leadership Conference.

DEADLINE: March

PROVIDER: American Foreign Services Association (AFSA)

WEBSITE: www.afsa.org/essay-contest

AXA Achievement Community Award

ELIGIBLE APPLICANT: Seniors

OTHER ELIGIBILITY: Citizen or legal resident of the U.S. or Puerto Rico who will attend an accredited 2 year or 4 year college in the U.S.

OVERVIEW: An annual award program for students who demonstrate outstanding achievement in their school, community or workplace. Students create a student profile and answer essay questions. Special award consideration will be given to students who empowered society to mitigate risk through education or action in areas such as financial, environmental, health, safety or climate change.

AWARD: $2,500. Up to 12 awards per AXA Advisors branch office.

DEADLINE: February

PROVIDER: AXA Foundation

WEBSITE: www.scholarshipamerica.org/axa-community

AXA Achievement Scholarship

ELIGIBLE APPLICANT: Seniors

OTHER ELIGIBILITY: Citizen or legal resident of the U.S. or Puerto Rico who will attend an accredited 2 year or 4 year college in the U.S.

OVERVIEW: An annual scholarship for students who demonstrate outstanding achievement in their school, community or workplace. Students create a student profile and answer essay questions. Special consideration will be given to students who empowered society to mitigate risk through education or action in areas such as financial, environmental, health, safety or climate change. Judges select one finalist from each state, District of Columbia and Puerto Rico, then select the top 10 finalists.

AWARD: $10,000 for 52 finalists. Additional $15,000 for top 10 finalists.

DEADLINE: Refer to the website for the next application cycle.

PROVIDER: AXA Foundation

WEBSITE: www.scholarshipamerica.org/axa-achievement

Ayn Rand Anthem Essay Contest

ELIGIBLE APPLICANT: Grades 9-10

OTHER ELIGIBILITY: Students anywhere in the world.

OVERVIEW: An essay (600-1,200 words) contest to educate students about the novel Anthem written by Ayn Rand. Students choose from one of three topics. The essays will be judged on the student's ability to argue and justify his/her viewpoint. Judges will select winners based on writing that is clear, articulate and well organized.

AWARD: $2,000 for the winner. $500 for the next 5 winners. $200 for the next 10 winners. $50 for the next 45 winners. $30 for the next 175 winners.

DEADLINE: March 25, 2016. Refer to the website for the next contest.

PROVIDER: Ayn Rand Institute

WEBSITE: www.aynrand.org/students/essay-contests#anthem-1

Ayn Rand Atlas Shrugged Essay Contest

ELIGIBLE APPLICANT: Seniors

OTHER ELIGIBILITY: Students anywhere in the world.

OVERVIEW: An essay (800-1,600 words) contest to educate students about the novel Atlas Shrugged written by Ayn Rand. Students must choose from one of three topics. Essays will be judged on a student's ability to argue and justify his/her viewpoint. Judges will select winners based on writing that is clear, articulate and well organized.

AWARD: $20,000 for the winner. $2,000 for the next 3 winners. $1,000 for the next 5 winners. $100 for the next 25 winncrs. $50 for the next 50 winners.

DEADLINE: April 28, 2017.

PROVIDER: Ayn Rand Institute

WEBSITE: www.aynrand.org/students/essay-contests# atlasshrugged-1

Ayn Rand The Fountainhead Essay Contest

ELIGIBLE APPLICANT: Grades 11-12

OTHER ELIGIBILITY: Students anywhere in the world.

OVERVIEW: An essay (800-1,600 words) contest to educate students about the novel The Fountainhead written by Ayn Rand. Students must choose from one of three topics. Essays will be judged on a student's ability to argue and justify his/her viewpoint. Judges will select winners based on writing that is clear, articulate and well organized.

AWARD: $10,000 for the winner. $2,000 for the next 5 winners. $1,000 for the next 10 winners. $100 for the next 45 winners. $50 for the next 175 winners.

DEADLINE: April 29, 2016. Refer to the website for the next contest.

PROVIDER: Ayn Rand Institute

WEBSITE: www.aynrand.org/students/essay-contests#the fountainhead-1

Barbara Mandigo Kelly Peace Poetry Awards

ELIGIBILE APPLICANT: Grades 9-12

OTHER ELIGIBILITY: Students attending high school anywhere in the world.

OVERVIEW: An annual poetry contest about peace. Students may submit up to three poems (maximum 30 lines per poem). Poems must be original and unpublished.

AWARD: $200 for the winner. Additional awards may be given for Honorable Mentions.

DEADLINE: April

PROVIDER: Nuclear Age Peace Foundation

WEBSITE: www.peacecontests.org

Bluetooth Breakthrough Award

ELIGIBLE APPLICANT: Grades 9-12

OTHER ELIGIBILITY: Students worldwide, with exception for certain countries.

OVERVIEW: An annual technology contest. There are several categories and experience levels including a student level. The student level is intended to recognize and encourage young innovators and inventors to work with Bluetooth technology on school projects, community service projects or as a hobby. Refer to the website for the contest rules and requirements.

AWARD: $5,000 for the student winner.

DEADLINE: November

PROVIDER: Bluetooth SIG Inc.

WEBSITE: www.bluetooth.com/news-events/awards

Brower Youth Awards

ELIGIBLE APPLICANT: Grades 9-12

OTHER ELIGIBILITY: Students in North America including the U.S. and Canada.

OVERVIEW: Earth Island Institute developed The New Leaders Initiative program to recognize environmental youth leaders. Judges focus on leaders of groups and group efforts rather than on individual efforts. Semi-finalists will be interviewed via Skype to determine the winners.

AWARD: $3,000 for 6 winners along with a short film about their work and an expense-paid trip to San Francisco.

DEADLINE: Refer to the website for the next application cycle.

PROVIDER: Earth Island Institute

WEBSITE: www.broweryouthawards.org/apply

BusinessPlanToday Annual Scholarship

ELIGIBLE APPLICANT: Seniors

OTHER ELIGIBILITY: Students who will attend college in the Fall on a full-time basis.

OVERVIEW: An award to the student who drafts the best business plan executive summary. Judges will consider the originality, creativity, uniqueness and persuasiveness of the executive summary. Students must wait until January 1st of their senior year to apply. The scholarship will apply to the Spring semester of the following year.

AWARD: $1,000 for the winner.

DEADLINE: December 15, 2016

PROVIDER: BusinessPlanToday

WEBSITE: https://resources.businessplantoday.com/bpt-annual-scholarship

Burger King General-Track Scholarship

ELIGIBLE APPLICANT: Seniors

OTHER ELIGIBILITY: 2.0 GPA. Students in the U.S., Canada and Puerto Rico who will attend an accredited two-year or four-year college in the U.S., Canada or Puerto Rico.

OVERVIEW: This annual scholarship program is intended for students who are not employees of Burger King. Students will be evaluated on academic record and participation in school and community activities. There is a separate scholarship for employees and dependents of employees of Burger King.

AWARD: $1,000. The number of awards varies.

DEADLINE: December

PROVIDER: Burger King McLamore Foundation

WEBSITE: http://bkmclamorefoundation.org/who-we-are/ burger-king-scholars-program

Carson Scholars Program

ELIGIBLE APPLICANT: Grades 9-11

OTHER ELIGIBILITY: 3.75 GPA. Students in the U.S. who will attend a four-year college.

OVERVIEW: An annual program to acknowledge and reward students who excel academically and are dedicated to community service. Students must be nominated by their schools. The application includes an essay and teacher recommendation. The school principal will be asked to verify the authenticity of the application. The award applies to a four-year college.

AWARD: $1,000. The number of awards varies.

DEADLINE: December

PROVIDER: Carson Scholars Fund

WEBSITE: www.carsonscholars.org/scholarships

CenturyLinkQuote Scholarship

ELIGIBLE APPLICANT: Seniors

OTHER ELIGIBILITY: U.S. citizen or permanent legal resident of the U.S. who will attend an accredited U.S. college in the Fall after high school graduation.

OVERVIEW: Students create an infographic to explain how the advancement of technology usage is leading to new career paths and leading more students away from traditional careers. Judges will consider the student's creativity, thoughtfulness and insight along with how well they promoted their post.

AWARD: $1,000 for the winner

DEADLINE: June 15, 2016.

PROVIDER: CenturyLinkQuote.com

WEBSITE: www.centurylinkquote.com/scholarship/rules

Christopher Reeve Service Award

ELIGIBLE APPLICANT: Grades 9-12

OTHER ELIGIBILITY: Student must be nominated.

OVERVIEW: An annual award is presented in honor of actor and activist Christopher Reeve to a student who demonstrates tremendous courage, compassion and caring in serving his or her community. Students must be nominated for consideration. The nomination form is not available to the public.

AWARD: $1,000 for the winner.

DEADLINE: Annually during Fall.

PROVIDER: The Heart of America Foundation

WEBSITE: www.heartofamerica.org/our-programs

Coca-Cola Scholars Scholarship

ELIGIBLE APPLICANT: Seniors

OTHER ELIGIBILITY: 3.0 GPA. Students attending high school in the U.S. who intend to enroll in an accredited U.S. college.

OVERVIEW: This annual prestigious scholarship recognizes students who excel academically and are actively involved in school activities. Judges look for students who are well rounded, passionate, intelligent, service-oriented, and committed to improving their community. Students submit an application online. 2,200 applicants are selected as Semifinalists and they submit additional materials, such as essays and official transcript, for consideration. 250 applicants are then selected as Regional Semifinalists. The finalists (scholars) are selected after interviews.

AWARD: $20,000 for 150 Scholars. A minimum of $1,000 for 100 Regional Finalists.

DEADLINE: October

PROVIDER: Coca Cola Scholars Foundation

WEBSITE: www.coca-colascholarsfoundation.org/applicants/ #programs

College Jump Start Scholarship

ELIGIBLE APPLICANT: Grades 10-12

OTHER ELIGIBILITY: U.S. citizen or legal resident of the U.S. who will attend an accredited U.S. college or trade school.

OVERVIEW: A merit-based competition offered twice a year. Students apply online and include a personal statement essay of 250 or less words. Judges select the winner based on the application and personal statement.

AWARD: $1,000. The number of awards varies.

DEADLINE: October 17 and April 15 of each year.

PROVIDER: College JumpStart Scholarship

WEBSITE: www.jumpstart-scholarship.net

Comcast Leaders and Achievers Scholarship

ELIGIBLE APPLICANT: Seniors

OTHER ELIGIBILITY: 2.8 GPA. Students attending high school in a community served or approved by Comcast. Students planning to attend an accredited non-profit college or vocational/technical school in the U.S.

OVERVIEW: This annual program recognizes students for high academic, leadership and community service achievements. Students must be nominated by their high school principal or guidance counselor for scholarship consideration. The principal or guidance counselor can request the eligibility requirements and a nomination form from Comcast at comcast@applyists.com or 1-855-670-4787. Students with parents who are employed by Comcast or its subsidiaries and affiliates are not eligible.

AWARD: $1,000, but additional amounts may be provided. The number of awards varies.

DEADLINE: December

PROVIDER: Comcast Foundation

WEBSITE: http://corporate.comcast.com/images/Leaders-and-Achievers-Fact-Sheet2.pdf

Common Knowledge Scholarship Foundation

ELIGIBLE APPLICANT: Grades 9-12

OTHER ELIGIBILITY: Students attending high school in the U.S.

OVERVIEW: This foundation offers a variety of scholarship quizzes throughout the year. Students receive 500 points for every correct answer and lose one point for every second it takes to answer the question. The timer starts as soon as the browser loads the question and stops when the student clicks submit. It then repeats the process for the next question. Students with the highest scores at the end of each competition win. Students register once on the website and receive notification of quizzes throughout the year. Awards may be used at any college in the U.S.

AWARD: $250 to $2,500. The number of awards varies.

DEADLINE: Periodic competitions.

PROVIDER: Common Knowledge Scholarship Foundation

WEBSITE: www.cksf.org/index.cfm?Page=Scholarships

Create-A-Greeting-Card Scholarship Contest

ELIGIBLE APPLICANT: Grades 9-12

OTHER ELIGIBILITY: U.S. citizen or legal resident. This includes American Samoa, Guam, the Commonwealth of the Northern Mariana Islands, the U.S. Virgin Islands and Puerto Rico.

OVERVIEW: An annual art contest. Students submit an original photo, artwork or computer graphic for the front of a greeting card, such as a holiday or birthday card. Up to 100 designs will be posted to The Gallery Collection website for public voting every month. The 10 designs with most votes for each month move into the next round. Then the top 5 designs with the most votes along with 5 designs selected by judges enter the final round. The judges then select the winner.

AWARD: $10,000 for the winner.

DEADLINE: February. Refer to the website for the next contest.

PROVIDER: Prudent Publishing Company Inc/The Gallery Collection

WEBSITE: www.gallerycollection.com/greeting-cards-scholarship.htm

Davidson Fellows Scholarship

ELIGIBLE APPLICANT: Grades 9-12

OTHER ELIGIBILITY: U.S. citizen or permanent resident living in the U.S. or at a U.S. military base.

OVERVIEW: This prestigious annual scholarship program recognizes students who completed a significant piece of work in one of the high school categories. The categories for high school students are STEM (Science, Technology, Engineering and Math) and Humanities (Literature, Music and Philosophy). Judges look for projects that are at a college graduate level.

AWARD: $50,000, $25,000 or $10,000 for each recipient as determined by the judges. Approximately 20 recipients receive awards.

DEADLINE: February

PROVIDER: Davidson Institute for Talent Development

WEBSITE: www.davidsongifted.org/fellows

Delete Cyberbullying Scholarship Award

ELIGIBLE APPLICANT: Grades 10-12

OTHER ELIGIBILITY: U.S. citizen or permanent resident living in the U.S. who will attend an accredited U.S. college.

OVERVIEW: A stop online harassment project to get students committed to deleting cyberbullying. Students write an essay (500 words or less) on one of two topics. The essays will be judged on creativity, content and a commitment to the cause of deleting cyberbullying.

AWARD: $1,000 to 1 recipient.

DEADLINE: June 30, 2016

PROVIDER: Delete Cyberbullying

WEBSITE: www.deletecyberbullying.org/scholarship

Denny's Hungry for Education Scholarship/ Magic Johnson Foundation

ELIGIBLE APPLICANT: Grades 9-12

OTHER ELIGIBILITY: 2.5 GPA. U.S. citizen or permanent resident attending high school in the U.S. or Puerto Rico. All students are eligible to apply regardless of race, color, religion or nationality.

OVERVIEW: Denny's and the Magic Johnson Foundation have partnered to offer this annual scholarship. The application requires an essay (up to 300 words). The essay topic is "How Denny's can impact childhood hunger in their local communities?" Grades and academic performance will serve as indicators of potential, but judges place an emphasis on the essay. Applicants must apply through the Denny's scholarship website.

AWARD: $1,000 for 5 winners.

DEADLINE: Refer to website for the next application cycle.

PROVIDER: Denny's & Magic Johnson Foundation

WEBSITE: https://dennysscholarships.versaic.com/login

Digital Privacy Scholarship

ELIGIBLE APPLICANT: Grades 9-12

OTHER ELIGIBILITY: U.S. citizen or legal resident living in the U.S.

OVERVIEW: The scholarship is intended to help students understand why they should be careful about what they post on social media. Students apply online with a personal statement about digital privacy. Ten applicants are selected as finalists and write an essay (500-1,000 words) about digital privacy. Judges select the winner based on the essay content and creativity.

AWARD: $1,000 for 1 winner.

DEADLINE: June 30, 2016

PROVIDER: Digital Responsibility

WEBSITE: www.digitalresponsibility.org/digital-privacy-scholarship

DNA Day Essay Contest

ELIGIBLE APPLICANT: Grades 9-12

OTHER ELIGIBILITY: Students anywhere in the world.

OVERVIEW: An annual science essay (up to 750 words) contest to encourage students to learn about genetics. The 2016 essay prompt is "Choose a genetic test for a condition or disease that does not cause symptoms until adulthood. Describe how the test works and how certain the test results are. Then, either defend or refute the ASHG's position statement on pediatric genetic testing, "Adolescents should be encouraged to defer predictive or pre-dispositional testing for adult-onset conditions until adulthood because of the complexity of the potential impact of the information at formative life stages." Refer to the website for the annual essay prompt and additional submission instructions.

AWARD: $1,000 for winner. $600 for second place. $400 for third place. $100 for 10 Honorable Mentions.

DEADLINE: March 11, 2016. Refer to the website for the next contest.

PROVIDER: The American Society of Human Genetics (ASHG)

WEBSITE: www.ashg.org/education/dnaday.shtml

Don't Text and Drive Scholarship

ELIGIBLE APPLICANT: Grades 9-12

OTHER ELIGIBILITY: U.S. citizen or legal resident living in the U.S.

OVERVIEW: A scholarship to help students understand the risks of texting while driving. Students submit a personal statement about texting and driving. The top ten finalists write an essay (500-1,000 words) about texting and driving. Judges select the winner on the essay content and creativity.

AWARD: $1,000 for the winner.

DEADLINE: September 30, 2016

PROVIDER: Digital Responsibility

WEBSITE: www.digitalresponsibility.org/dont-text-and-drive-scholarship

Doodle for Google

ELIGIBLE APPLICANT: Grades 9-12

OTHER ELIGIBILITY: U.S. citizens attending high school in the U.S., Puerto Rico or Guam or children of military personnel abroad.

OVERVIEW: An annual art contest. Students create a doodle that incorporates the letters Google. Refer to the website for the annual doodle theme. The doodles will be judged on artistic skill, creativity and theme. The public will have an opportunity to vote on the best 53 doodles to help decide the five National Finalists, but a panel of judges ultimately select the winners.

AWARD: $30,000 for the winner. $5,000 for 4 National Finalists.

DEADLINE: December

PROVIDER: Google

WEBSITE: www.google.com/doodle4google/index.html

DuPont Challenge Science Essay Competition

ELIGIBLE APPLICANT: Grades 9-12

OTHER ELIGIBILITY: Students in U.S., Canada and its territories.

OVERVIEW: An annual essay (700-1,000 words) contest to encourage students to research science, technology, engineering and math (STEM) and express their ideas about how science can help the global population. Students select from one of four categories; food, energy, environment and innovation. Refer to the website for the contest rules.

AWARD: 5,000 savings bond and additional prizes for the winner. $3,000 savings bond and additional prizes for second place. $1,000 savings bond and additional prizes for third place. $200 savings bond for Honorable Mentions.

DEADLINE: February

PROVIDER: DuPont

WEBSITE: http://thechallenge.dupont.com/essay/students-intro

E-waste Scholarship

ELIGIBLE APPLICANT: Grades 9-12

OTHER ELIGIBILITY: U.S. citizen or legal resident living in the U.S.

OVERVIEW: This scholarship is intended to help students understand the impact of discarding electronics (also known as e-waste) and what can be done to reduce e-waste. Students apply online with a personal statement about e-waste. Ten applicants are selected as finalists and write an essay (500-1,000 words) about e-waste. Judges select the winner based on the essay content and creativity.

AWARD: $1,000 for the winner.

DEADLINE: April 30, 2016

PROVIDER: Digital Responsibility

WEBSITE: www.digitalresponsibility.org/ewaste-scholarship

Executive Women International (EWI) Scholarship

ELIGIBLE APPLICANT: Seniors

OTHER ELIGIBILITY: Compete at local EWI chapter.

OVERVIEW: A program to assist women pursue a degree at an accredited four-year college in U.S. or Canada. Students must be nominated by their school and compete at the local EWI chapter. There are 51 local chapters in U.S. and Canada. Refer to the website for locations. Local chapters submit winners to the national organization for a chance to win a scholarship. Judges select winners based on academic achievement, leadership, good citizenship and extra-curricular activities.

AWARD: $1,000 to $5,000. The number of awards varies. Local chapters may provide additional awards.

DEADLINE: December

PROVIDER: Executive Women International (EWI)

WEBSITE: www.ewiconnect.com

Foot Locker Scholar Athletes

ELIGIBLE APPLICANT: Seniors

OTHER ELIGIBILITY: 3.0 GPA. U.S citizen or permanent resident. Students who will attend an accredited four-year college in the Fall after high school graduation.

OVERVIEW: This annual scholarship program rewards outstanding student athletes who demonstrate strong leadership skills on their sports teams, in their school and within the communities and who excel academically. Students do not need to be on a varsity team.

AWARD: $20,000 for 20 winners. One of the winners will also be selected for the Ken C. Hicks $5,000 scholarship.

DEADLINE: December

PROVIDER: Foot Locker

WEBSITE: www.footlockerscholarathletes.com

FRA Americanism Essay Contest

ELIGIBLE APPLICANT: Grades 9-12

OTHER ELIGIBILITY: Students sponsored by an FRA member or branch.

OVERVIEW: An annual essay contest to promote the spirit of Americanism and patriotism. The 2016 essay prompt is "What does the U.S. flag stand for?" Students submit an essay (up to 350 words) through their local FRA branch or member. Local winners compete at the regional level. Regional winners compete at the national level. Refer to the website for FRA branches.

AWARD: $5,000 for the national winner. The top 3 essays in each grade are awarded $2,500 for 1st place, $1,500 for 2nd place and $1,000 for 3rd place.

DEADLINE: December

PROVIDER: Fleet Reserve Association (FRA)

WEBSITE: www.fra.org/fra/Web/FRA_Docs/EssayContest/Essay-Rules.pdf

From Failure to Promise Essay Contest

ELIGIBLE APPLICANT: Seniors

OTHER ELIGIBILITY: 2.5 GPA. Students who will attend an accredited college in the U.S., Canada or Mexico.

OVERVIEW: A essay (at least 1,500 words) contest on the author's autobiography "From Failure to Promise: 360 Degrees." The essay must address all three essay prompts, which are posted on the website. The essays will be judged on originality, quality of research and presentation.

AWARD: $10,000 for the winner. $500 for 3 Honorable Mentions.

DEADLINE: July 31, 2016

PROVIDER: Doctor C. Moore & Associates, Inc.

WEBSITE: www.fromfailuretopromise.com/#!essay-scholarship-contest--html/cfvg

FRRF High School Student Scholarship Essay Contest

ELIGIBLE APPLICANT: Seniors

OTHER ELIGIBILITY: U.S. or Canadian citizen. Students who enroll full-time at an accredited two-year or four-year college.

OVERVIEW: An annual essay contest about a topic selected by the Freedom from Religion Foundation. Refer to the website in February for the annual essay prompt and contest rules.

AWARD: $200 to $3,000. The number of awards varies.

DEADLINE: Refer to the website for the next contest and deadline.

PROVIDER: Freedom from Religion Foundation

WEBSITE: https://ffrf.org/outreach/ffrf-student-scholarship-essay-contests

Gen and Kelly Tanabe Scholarship

ELIGIBLE APPLICANT: Grades 9-12

OTHER ELIGIBILITY: U.S. legal resident.

OVERVIEW: A merit-based scholarship program to assist students further their education. Students submit a personal statement (up to 250 words) about why they deserve to win or describing their academic or career goals or on any topic of their choice. The scholarship program typically runs every six months.

AWARD: $1,000 for the winner.

DEADLINE: July 31, 2016. Refer to the website for the next deadline.

PROVIDER: Gen and Kelly Tanabe

WEBSITE: www.genkellyscholarship.com

Google Science Fair Awards

ELIGIBLE APPLICANT: Grades 9-12

OTHER ELIGIBILITY: Students from around the world.

OVERVIEW: An annual global online science competition where students submit a science project on topics, such as biology, chemistry, engineering, math, computer science, food science, physics, flora & fauna and behavioral and social science. The project must follow the technical, creative, and legal requirements established by the science fair. Projects are judged in one of the two age groups (13-15 and 16-18). Students can enter as individuals or teams. Refer to the website for additional information.

AWARD: $50,000 for the winner. Additional awards include $25,000, $10,000 and $5,000 for certain categories.

DEADLINE: Refer to the website for the next competition.

PROVIDER: Google

WEBSITE: www.googlesciencefair.com/en

Gloria Barron Prize for Young Heroes

ELIGIBLE APPLICANT: Grades 9-12

OTHER ELIGIBILITY: Students residing in the U.S. or Canada. Students working on a service project within the past 12 months.

OVERVIEW: This annual service challenge program is intended to encourage students to get involved and make a significant difference to people and the environment. Students must be working as leaders of their service work. The application includes an essay (up to 1,500 words) and a letter from a lead reference.

AWARD: $5,000. 15 awards are provided.

DEADLINE: April

PROVIDER: Gloria Barron Prize for Young Heroes

WEBSITE: www.barronprize.org

Hays C. Kirby Memorial Scholarship Contest

ELIGIBLE APPLICANT: Grades 11-12

OTHER ELIGIBILITY: U.S. citizen who will attend an accredited U.S. college.

OVERVIEW: An annual essay (1,500-2,000 words) contest to educate students about civics, patriotism, citizenship, and what it means to be an American. The 2016 essay prompt is "If Not For Them, Where Would We Be?" Judges will select winners based on their creativity, theme development, clarity of ideas and writing mechanics.

AWARD: $5,000 for the winner. $2,500 for second place. $1,000 for third place.

DEADLINE: March

PROVIDER: Joe Foss Institute

WEBSITE: www.joefossinstitute.org/jfi-scholarship-program

Herff Jones Believe in You Scholarship & Principal's Award

ELIGIBLE APPLICANT: Seniors

OTHER ELIGIBILITY: Students attending high school in the U.S., Puerto Rico, Virgin Islands and Canada.

OVERVIEW: A scholarship to recognize high achieving student leaders. The high school principal nominates one student who excels academically and demonstrates strong leadership skills. Judges consider academics, SAT/ACT scores, involvement in school and community activities, work experience and the response to the essay prompt.

AWARD: $12,000 for the national winner. $8,500 for second place. $5,000 for third place. $2,000 for 47 finalists.

DEADLINE: February 8, 2016. Refer to website for the next nomination deadline.

PROVIDER: Herff Jones

WEBSITE: www.herffjones.com/biuscholarship

Humane Educational Network "A Voice for Animals" Contest

ELIGIBLE APPLICANT: Grades 9-12

OTHER ELIGIBILITY: Students attending high school anywhere in the world.

OVERVIEW: An annual contest with awards for categories in video, essay and blog. Refer to the website for the annual contest rules and requirements. Entries must be submitted through the form on the website.

AWARD: Varies

DEADLINE: March

PROVIDER: Humane Education Network

WEBSITE: www.hennet.org/contest

Humanity Rising Service Challenge Cash Scholarship

ELIGIBLE APPLICANT: Grades 9-12

OTHER ELIGIBILITY: 2.5 GPA. U.S. citizen or permanent resident.

OVERVIEW: A service challenge to encourage students to get involved and make a positive impact in their communities. Students complete a service challenge and submit the required service project information for scholarship consideration. There are ten featured causes and students can volunteer at a nonprofit organization in one of these causes, complete some of the recommended service activities or create their own service project. A teacher or supervisor must verify the project and completed hours.

AWARD: $500 to $2,000. The number of awards varies.

DEADLINE: Refer to website

PROVIDER: Humane Education Network

WEBSITE: www.humanityrising.org/pages/challenge

Hunter Garner Scholarship

ELIGIBLE APPLICANT: Grades 11-12

OTHER ELIGIBILITY: U.S. citizen or legal resident.

OVERVIEW: An annual memorial scholarship to help students understand the risks of distracted driving and encourage safe driving habits. Students create a short film (25-55 seconds) about the topic. The film can be a video which includes yourself or a group, a cartoon, a music video using approved songs or any other type of film. Entries can be from individuals or teams (maximum of 4 members). The winning video will be distributed nationally to 1,600 TV stations. Refer to the website for additional information.

AWARD: $5,000 for the winner. $2,000 for 2nd place. $1,000 for 3rd place.

DEADLINE: April

PROVIDER: Project Yellow Light

WEBSITE: www.projectyellowlight.com/about

Image Cup Contests

ELIGIBLE APPLICANT: Age 16 and up.

OTHER ELIGIBILITY: Students worldwide, with exception for certain countries.

OVERVIEW: An annual technology contest. There is a beginner, medium and advanced level. Students can enter as individual or teams. Interns and employees of Microsoft or its subsidiaries are not eligible. Refer to the website for the contests and rules.

AWARD: up to $50,000. The amount and number of awards varies by contest.

DEADLINE: Varies by contest. Refer to the website.

PROVIDER: Microsoft

WEBSITE: www.imaginecup.com/category/index#

Insureon Small Business Scholarship

ELIGIBLE APPLICANT: Seniors

OTHER ELIGIBILITY: U.S. citizen or legal resident who will enroll full-time in a two-year or four-year college in the U.S.

OVERVIEW: A contest to promote small businesses. Students write an essay (500-700 words) on a topic that is posted on the website. The Spring 2016 topic is "What is your favorite small business and why?" The contest is currently running three times a year.

AWARD: $2,500 for two winners.

DEADLINE: Refer to the website for the contests and deadlines.

PROVIDER: Insureon

WEBSITE: www.insureon.com/insureonu/small-business-scholarship

IP Video Contest

ELIGIBLE APPLICANT: Grades 9-12

OTHER ELIGIBILITY: Students in the U.S. and its territories.

OVERVIEW: An annual video contest about the patent system. Students create an original short video (no more than 90 seconds) about the importance of the patent system. They select from one of the topics posted on the website. Two winners are selected from each category (13-15 years old and 16-18 years old). One winner per age category is decided by public voting and the other by the Foundation's Board of Directors.

AWARD: $5,000 for 2 winners in the 13-15 years old category. $5,000 for 2 winners in the 16-18 year old category.

DEADLINE: August

PROVIDER: Intellectual Property Owners (IPO) Education Foundation

WEBSITE: www.ipvideocontest.com

John F. Kennedy Profile in Courage Essay Contest

ELIGIBLE APPLICANT: Grades 9-12

OTHER ELIGIBILITY: Students attending high school in the U.S.

OVERVIEW: An annual contest to encourage students to research about politics and political courage. Students write an essay (700-1,000 words) about an act of political courage by a U.S. elected official who served during or after 1956. The official could be from the local, state or national level, but cannot be John Kennedy, Robert Kennedy or Edward Kennedy. The essay will be judged on content and presentation.

AWARD: $10,000 for the winner. $1,000 for 2nd place. $500 for up to 5 more finalists.

DEADLINE: January

PROVIDER: John F. Kennedy Library Foundation

WEBSITE: www.jfklibrary.org/Education/Profile-in-Courage-Essay-Contest.aspx

Knights of Pythias High School Poster/Visual Arts Contest

ELIGIBLE APPLICANT: Grades 9-12

OTHER ELIGIBILITY: Students attending high school in the U.S. and Canada.

OVERVIEW: An annual poster contest. The 2016 theme is "Stay Alive, Don't Text and Drive." Students submit the poster through a local Knights of Pythias lodge. Refer to the website for locations. The local lodge will enter its winner in the state competition. The state winner is entered into the national competition.

AWARD: $1,000 for the winner. $500 for second place. $250 for third place. $100 for fourth through eighth place.

DEADLINE: Contact the local lodge.

PROVIDER: The Supreme Lodge Knights of Pythias

WEBSITE: www.pythias.org/index.php?option=com_wrapper&view=wrapper&Itemid=55

Letters About Literature Contest

ELIGIBLE APPLICANT: Grades 9-12

OTHER ELIGIBILITY: U.S. citizen or legal resident.

OVERVIEW: An annual reading and writing contest. Students read a book, poem or speech and write a personal letter to the author about how the book, poem or speech affected them. Letters are judged on audience, purpose, grammar and originality on a state and national level.

AWARD: $1,000 for the national winner. $200 for one or more Honorable Mentions.

DEADLINE: Refer to the website for the contest and deadline.

PROVIDER: Library of Congress

WEBSITE: http://read.gov/letters

Life Lessons Scholarship

ELIGIBLE APPLICANT: Age 17 and up.

OTHER ELIGIBILITY: Death of a parent or legal guardian. U.S. citizen or legal resident who has been accepted to a college in the U.S. or Puerto Rico.

OVERVIEW: A scholarship program for students who experienced the death of a parent or legal guardian. The application is submitted with an essay (no more than 500 words) or video (no more than 3 minutes) describing the financial and emotional challenges experienced due to the death of a parent or legal guardian and how inadequate or no life insurance impacted the situation.

AWARD: $15,000 to 4 recipients. $12,500 for 2 recipients. $10,000 for 2 recipients. $8,000 for 10 recipients. $5,000 for 13 recipients.

DEADLINE: February

PROVIDER: Life Happens

WEBSITE: www.lifehappens.org/life-lessons-scholarship-program

Mediacom World Class Scholars Scholarship

ELIGIBLE APPLICANT: Seniors

OTHER ELIGIBILITY: Students living in a community served by Mediacom. Students planning to attend a two-year or four-year accredited college or vocational/technical school in the U.S.

OVERVIEW: An annual program to recognize students for high academic, leadership and community service achievements. The application includes an essay (about 500 words). Students with parents who are employed by Mediacom are not eligible. Refer to the website for a list of eligible communities.

AWARD: $1,000. The number of awards varies.

DEADLINE: February

PROVIDER: Mediacom

WEBSITE: www.mediacomworldclass.com

MyProjectorLamps Scholarship

ELIGIBLE APPLICANT: Seniors

OTHER ELIGIBILITY: 3.0 GPA. Students attending a U.S. school.

OVERVIEW: A biannual essay (one page) contest to encourage students to think about ways to use multimedia and data visualization in the classroom, explore modern teaching methods and suggest ideas for visual and interactive presentation to improve knowledge retention.

AWARD: $500 for two winners.

DEADLINE: Refer to the website for the biannual contests.

PROVIDER: MyProjectorLamps

WEBSITE: www.myprojectorlamps.com/scholarships.html

National Merit Scholarship

ELIGIBLE APPLICANT: Juniors (exceptions apply)

OTHER ELIGIBILITY: Taking PSAT/NMSQT. U.S. citizen. Students enrolling in college full time in Fall following high school graduation.

OVERVIEW: Students are automatically entered when they take the Preliminary SAT/National Merit Scholarship Qualifying Test (PSAT/NMSQT) in the year specified by their high school. Approximately 50,000 of the highest scores are recognized as Commended Students or Semi-Finalist. Commended students do not advance in the competition, but may become candidates for special scholarships sponsored by corporations. Approximately 16,000 semi-finalists receive an application for further advancement. Approximately 15,000 advance to the Final round. Approximately 7,400 are selected for one of three Merit Scholarships.

AWARD: $2,500 National Merit Scholarship or another amount as a Corporate-Sponsored Merit Scholarship or College Sponsored Scholarship.

DEADLINE: Typically taken in October

PROVIDER: National Merit Scholarship Corporation

WEBSITE: www.nationalmerit.org/nmsp.php

National WWII Museum Essay Contest

ELIGIBLE APPLICANT: Grades 9-12

OTHER ELIGIBILITY: Students attending high school in the U.S., its territories or military bases.

OVERVIEW: An annual essay (up to 1,000 words) contest to encourage students to research WWII. Students write an essay about a topic posted on the website. The first 500 properly formatted essay submissions are considered for an award.

AWARD: $1,000 for the winner. $750 for second place. $500 for third place.

DEADLINE: March

PROVIDER: The National WWII Museum

WEBSITE: www.nationalww2museum.org/learn/education/for-students/essay-contests

NRA Civil Rights Defense Fund Youth Essay Contest

ELIGIBLE APPLICANT: Grades 9-12

OTHER ELIGIBILITY: Students attending high school in the U.S.

OVERVIEW: An annual essay (1,000 words) contest on the second amendment. The theme for the essay is "What Does the Second Amendment Mean to You?"

AWARD: $1,000 for the winner. $600 for second place. $200 for third place. $100 for fourth place.

DEADLINE: December

PROVIDER: The National Rifle Association Civil Rights Defense Fund

WEBSITE: www.nradefensefund.org/contests-scholarships.aspx

Odenza Marketing Group Scholarship

ELIGIBLE APPLICANT: Seniors

OTHER ELIGIBILITY: 2.5 GPA. Citizen of the U.S. or Canada. Students attending an accredited college in the U.S. or Canada in the Fall after high school graduation.

OVERVIEW: A contest typically offered twice a year. Students submit answers to essay questions on the online application.

AWARD: $500 for the winner.

DEADLINE: March

PROVIDER: Odenza Marketing Group

WEBSITE: www.odenzascholarships.com

Optimist International Essay Contest

ELIGIBLE APPLICANT: Grades 9-12

OTHER ELIGIBILITY: Students in the U.S., Canada and Caribbean. Awards are provided for college or trade school in the U.S., Canada or Caribbean.

OVERVIEW: An annual essay (700-800 words) contest to provide young people with the opportunity to express their opinions regarding the world. Refer to the website for the annual essay prompt. Students must submit the essay to their local Optimist club. If a local Club is not available, then the student may enter an At-Large contest. Local club winners advance to the District level to compete for a scholarship. Refer to the website for local Club contact information.

AWARD: Each District provides $2,500 for the winner.

DEADLINE: Refer to the website for the next contest.

PROVIDER: Optimist International

WEBSITE: www.optimist.org/e/member/scholarships3.cfm

Optimist International Oratorical Contest

ELIGIBLE APPLICANT: Grades 9-12

OTHER ELIGIBILITY: Students in the U.S., Canada and Caribbean. Awards are provided for college or trade school in the U.S., Canada or Caribbean.

OVERVIEW: An annual speech contest to provide young people with the opportunity to express their opinions regarding the world. Refer to the website for the annual topic. Students must enter through the local Club. The contest begins at the local Club level then proceeds to the Zone level and then the District level where contestants compete for a scholarship. Refer to the website for local Club contact information.

AWARD: Each District provides either $2,500 for 2 winners (one male and one female) or $2,500 for the winner, $1,500 for second place and $1,000 for third place.

DEADLINE: Refer to the website for the next contest.

PROVIDER: Optimist International

WEBSITE: www.optimist.org/e/member/scholarships4.cfm

ProofreadingServices.com Video Poetry Contest

ELIGIBLE APPLICANT: Seniors

OTHER ELIGIBILITY: Students attending high school anywhere in the world.

OVERVIEW: A poetry contest. Students write an original poem (no minimum or maximum length) and record it on video. The video must be posted on YouTube. Students may submit more than one entry.

AWARD: $500 for first place. $300 for second place. $100 for third place.

DEADLINE: February 29, 2016

PROVIDER: ProofreadingServices.com

WEBSITE: www.proofreadingservices.com/pages/scholarship

Power Poetry Slams Scholarships

ELIGIBLE APPLICANT: Grades 9-12

OTHER ELIGIBILITY: Students attending high school in the U.S. who will attend college in the U.S. or its territories.

OVERVIEW: Annual poetry contests are announced during the year. Students submit one poem per contest. There are no minimum or maximum words.

AWARD: $1,000 for the winner.

DEADLINE: Refer to the website for the contests and deadlines.

PROVIDER: Poetry Power

WEBSITE: www.powerpoetry.org/content/poetry-scholarships-power-poetry

Religious Liberty Essay Scholarship Contest

ELIGIBLE APPLICANT: Grades 11-12

OVERVIEW: An annual essay (800-1,200 words) contest about church-state issues. The essay topic is posted on the website. The essay is intended to encourage students to express a viewpoint on the religious liberty topic. Students require an advisor, such as a teacher, to authenticate their work. Essays will be judged on a student's mastery of the topic, depth of the content and writing skills.

AWARD: $2000 for the winner and a trip to Washington D.C. $1,000 for second place. $250 for third place.

DEADLINE: March

PROVIDER: Baptist Joint Committee for Religious Liberty

WEBSITE: http://bjconline.org/contest

ResumeCompanion.com Scholarship

ELIGIBLE APPLICANT: Seniors

OTHER ELIGIBILITY: Students worldwide who will enroll in college in the Fall after high school graduation.

OVERVIEW: An annual scholarship for students who create the best resume based on the life of any fictional or non-fictional character from TV, history, literature or myth.

AWARD: $1,000 for the winner.

DEADLINE: July

PROVIDER: ResumeCompanion.com

WEBSITE: www.resumecompanion.com/scholarship

Rocket55 Scholarship

ELIGIBLE APPLICANT: Seniors

OVERVIEW: An annual technology contest. For 2016, students write an essay (300-500 words) on one of three topics. The topics are (1) How is digital marketing different than or the same as traditional marketing? (2) What is the role of social media in overall business strategy? (3) What makes a website great?

AWARD: $1,000 for the winner.

DEADLINE: May 31, 2016. Refer to the website for subsequent contests and deadlines.

PROVIDER: Rocket55

WEBSITE: www.rocket55.com/scholarship/apply

Scholastic Art & Writing Awards

ELIGIBLE APPLICANT: Grades 9-12

OTHER ELIGIBILITY: Students attending high school in the U.S., Canada and American Schools abroad.

OVERVIEW: The Alliance for Young Artists & Writers in partnership with art institutes, colleges and other sponsors provide scholarships for art and writing. There are 11 writing and 17 art categories. Students upload their work on the website and mail a submission to the local program. Refer to the website for the local program addresses.

AWARD: Varies by category and sponsor.

DEADLINE: Refer to the website "deadline look-up" for information.

PROVIDER: Alliance for Young Artists & Writers

WEBSITE: www.artandwriting.org/the-awards/how-to-enter

Siemens Competition in Math, Science & Technology

ELIGIBLE APPLICANT: Grades 9-12

OTHER ELIGIBILITY: Students from around the world.

OVERVIEW: An annual research competition on science, math and technology. Students submit a research project as individuals or teams and compete at the regional and national level. Individual submissions must be from seniors. Team submissions can have a maximum of three members and no seniors. Individuals and teams are judged separately.

AWARD: $100,000 for individual and team winners. $50,000 for individual and team 2nd place winners. $40,000 for individual and team 3rd place winners. $30,000 for individual and team 4th place winners. $20,000 for individual and team 5th place winners. $10,000 for individual and team 6th place winners.

DEADLINE: Refer to the website for the next contest and deadline.

PROVIDER: Siemens Foundation

WEBSITE: www.siemens-foundation.org/programs/the-siemens-competition-in-math-science-technology

Signet Classics Student Scholarship Essay Contest

ELIGIBLE APPLICANT: Grades 11-12

OTHER ELIGIBILITY: Students attending high school in the U.S.

OVERVIEW: An annual essay contest. For 2016, students write an essay (2-3 double spaced pages) on the book "Little Women" and choose from one of the five topics posted on the website. The essay must be submitted by a high school English teacher on behalf of the student. The next essay contest will be on the book "The Tempest."

AWARD: $1,000 for five winners.

DEADLINE: April 14, 2016 for "Little Women". Refer to the website for the next contest and deadline.

PROVIDER: Penguin Publishing Group

WEBSITE: www.penguin.com/services-academic/essayhome

Spirit of Anne Frank Scholarship

ELIGIBLE APPLICANT: Seniors

OTHER ELIGIBILITY: U.S. students who will attend a four-year college.

OVERVIEW: An annual program to recognize students who carry on Anne Frank's message and legacy of hope, courage, peace, justice and equality. Students submit a personal essay (no more than 1,000 words) and two letters of recommendation with their online application. The essay should showcase the student's community activism and how he/she was inspired by Anne Frank. Judges will be looking for students who lead organizations, programs or events that address intolerance, prejudice and injustice in their communities.

AWARD: $10,000 for the winner. $5,000 for second place. Additional runners-up will receive an award.

DEADLINE: February

PROVIDER: The Anne Frank Center USA

WEBSITE: http://annefrank.com/about-the-awards

Stephen J. Brady Stop Hunger Scholarship

ELIGIBLE APPLICANT: Grades 9-12

OTHER ELIGIBILITY: U.S. citizen or permanent resident attending high school in the U.S.

OVERVIEW: An annual program to recognize students who are working to end hunger in their communities. Students must have performed unpaid volunteer services impacting hunger in the U.S. within the last 12 months.

AWARD: $5,000 per recipient. In addition, a matching grant of $5,000 in the recipient's name for the hunger-related charity of their choice. Up to 20 recipients are selected annually.

DEADLINE: December

PROVIDER: Sodexo Foundation

WEBSITE: www.sodexofoundation.org/hunger_us/scholarships/scholarships.asp

Swackhamer Disarmament Video Contest

ELIGIBLE APPLICANT: Grades 9-12

OTHER ELIGIBILITY: Students attending high school anywhere in the world.

OVERVIEW: An annual short video (90 seconds) contest about an aspect of nuclear disarmament. The annual topic is posted on the website.

AWARD: $500 for the winner. $300 for second place. $200 for third place. $100 for fourth place. $50 for fifth place.

DEADLINE: April

PROVIDER: Nuclear Age Peace Foundation

WEBSITE: www.peacecontests.org

The American Legion High School Oratorical National Contest Scholarship

ELIGIBLE APPLICANT: Grades 9-12

OTHER ELIGIBILITY: U.S. citizen or permanent resident enrolled in a U.S. high school who will attend a U.S. college.

OVERVIEW: An annual oration contest designed for students to develop a deeper understanding and appreciation for the U.S. Constitution. Students are presented with speaking challenges that teaches leadership, the history of U.S. laws, and an understanding of the rights, privileges and responsibilities of American citizenship. The contest begins at the local level. Winners advance through county, district, state and national levels.

AWARD: $18,000 for the winner. $16,000 for second place. $14,000 for third place. First round participants in the National level who don't advance receive $1,500. Second round participants in the National level who don't advance to Finals receive an additional $1,500.

NOTE: Scholarships may be awarded to participants by local posts, districts, counties and states during earlier levels of competition.

DEADLINE: Contests begin at the local level.

PROVIDER: The American Legion

WEBSITE: www.legion.org/scholarships/oratorical

The Christophers Annual Poster Contest for High School Students

ELIGIBLE APPLICANT: Grades 9-12

OTHER ELIGIBILITY: U.S. citizen or resident with a S.S. Number.

OVERVIEW: An annual poster contest. The 2016 theme is "One Person Can Make a Difference." Judges evaluate posters on impact, effectiveness in conveying the theme, originality and artistic skill.

AWARD: $1,000 for the winner. $500 for second place. $250 for third place. $100 for up to 5 Honorable Mentions.

DEADLINE: February

PROVIDER: The Christophers

WEBSITE: www.christophers.org/page.aspx?pid=274

The Joseph S. Rumbaugh Historical Oration Contest

ELIGIBLE APPLICANT: Grades 9-12

OTHER ELIGIBILITY: U.S. citizen or permanent resident enrolled in a U.S. high school who will attend a U.S. college.

OVERVIEW: An annual oration contest about the Revolutionary War. Students write and perform an original oration of 5-6 minutes about an event, personality, or document related to the Revolutionary War and show a relationship to America today. The contest begins at the local level. Winners advance through district, state and national levels. Applications are available from the local chapter of Sons of the American Revolution.

AWARD: $5,000 for the winner. $3,000 for second place. $2,000 for third place. All other National Finalists receive $400. All other National Contestants receive $200. Additional awards may be provided by the state society or district post.

DEADLINE: Contests begin at the local level.

PROVIDER: National Society of the Sons of the American Revolution

WEBSITE: www.sar.org/Youth/Oration_Contest

The Prudential Spirit of Community Awards

ELIGIBLE APPLICANT: Grades 9-12

OTHER ELIGIBILITY: U.S. citizen or legal resident. Students who volunteer for a service activity within the past year.

OVERVIEW: An annual program to recognize students for their involvement in community service. Students are nominated by schools are organizations participating in this program. Judges select the top high school volunteer from each state and Washington D.C. A panel of judges then reviews the 51 State High School Honorees and selects five High School National Honorees.

AWARD: $6,000 for 5 National Honorees and $5,000 to the non-profit charitable organization of their choice. $1,000 for State High School Honorees.

DEADLINE: November

PROVIDER: Prudential

WEBSITE: http://spirit.prudential.com/view/page/soc/14830

The Tribute to the Rescuers Essay Contest

ELIGIBLE APPLICANT: Grades 9-12

OVERVIEW: An annual essay contest to educate students about the holocaust and the brave people who jeopardized their lives for the benefit of others. Students write an essay (750-1,000 words) about an individual or group that shows moral courage and connect it to the Holocaust if it is a non-Holocaust example. Students compete in one of two categories (grades 9-10 or grades 11-12).

AWARD: $800 for the winner of grades 9-10 and of grades 11-12. $550 for second place in grades 9-10 and in grades 11-12. $300 for third place in grades 9-10 and in grades 11-12. $100 for honorable mentions.

DEADLINE: February

PROVIDER: Institute for Holocaust Education

WEBSITE: http://ihene.org/holocaust-essay-contest-for-hs

The Vegetarian Resource Group Scholarship

ELIGIBLE APPLICANT: Seniors

OTHER ELIGIBILITY: Students attending high school in the U.S. who plan to attend college in the U.S.

OVERVIEW: An annual award for students promoting vegetarianism in their schools and/or communities. Students submit an essay addressing 16 questions that are posted on the website along with their transcript and three recommendations.

AWARD: $10,000 for the winner. $5,000 for 2 second place winners.

DEADLINE: February

PROVIDER: The Vegetarian Resource Group

WEBSITE: www.vrg.org/student/scholar.htm

Unigo All About Education Scholarship

ELIGIBLE APPLICANT: Grades 9-12

OTHER ELIGIBILITY: U.S. citizen or legal resident.

OVERVIEW: This is one of the many scholarships that are offered throughout the year by Unigo. Students create a free Unigo account and submit a short essay (up to 250 words) for the question "How will a $3,000 scholarship for education make a difference in your life?" Judges select the winner based on the essay.

AWARD: $3,000 for the winner.

DEADLINE: April 30, 2016

PROVIDER: Unigo

WEBSITE: www.unigo.com/scholarships/our-scholarships/all-about-education-scholarship

Unigo Do-Over Scholarship

ELIGIBLE APPLICANT: Grades 9-12

OTHER ELIGIBILITY: U.S. citizen or legal resident.

OVERVIEW: This is one of the many scholarships that are offered throughout the year by Unigo. Students create a free Unigo account and submit a short essay (up to 250 words) for the question "If you could get one 'do-over' in life, what would it be and why?" Judges select the winner based on the essay.

AWARD: $1,500 for the winner.

DEADLINE: June 30, 2016

PROVIDER: Unigo

WEBSITE: www.unigo.com/scholarships/our-scholarships/do-over-scholarship

Unigo Education Matters Scholarship

ELIGIBLE APPLICANT: Grades 9-12

OTHER ELIGIBILITY: U.S. citizen or legal resident.

OVERVIEW: This is one of the many fun scholarships that are offered throughout the year by Unigo. Students create a free Unigo account and submit a short essay (up to 250 words) for the question "What would you say to someone who thinks education doesn't matter, or that college is a waste of time and money?" Judges select the winner based on the essay.

AWARD: $5,000 for the winner.

DEADLINE: November 30, 2016

PROVIDER: Unigo

WEBSITE: www.unigo.com/scholarships/our-scholarships/ education-matters-scholarship

Unigo Fifth Month Scholarship

ELIGIBLE APPLICANT: Grades 9-12

OTHER ELIGIBILITY: U.S. citizen or legal resident.

OVERVIEW: This is one of the many fun scholarships that are offered throughout the year by Unigo. Students create a free Unigo account and submit a short essay (up to 250 words) for the question "May is the fifth month of the year. Write a letter to the number five explaining why five is important. Be serious or be funny. Either way, here's a high five to you for being original." Judges select the winner based on the essay.

AWARD: $1,500 for the winner.

DEADLINE: May 31, 2016

PROVIDER: Unigo

WEBSITE: www.unigo.com/scholarships/our-scholarships/fifth-month-scholarship

Unigo Flavor of the Month Scholarship

ELIGIBLE APPLICANT: Grades 9-12

OTHER ELIGIBILITY: U.S. citizen or legal resident.

OVERVIEW: A fun scholarship offered by Unigo. Students create a free Unigo account and submit a short essay (up to 250 words) for the question "Summer and ice cream go hand-in-hand. In fact, July is National Ice Cream Month, and that's the inspiration behind this award. We think people are very similar to ice cream; some are nutty, others a little exotic, while some are very comforting. If you were an ice cream flavor, which would you be and why?" Judges select the winner based on the essay.

AWARD: $1,500 for the winner.

DEADLINE: July 31, 2016

PROVIDER: Unigo

WEBSITE: www.unigo.com/scholarships/our-scholarships/flavor-of-the-month-scholarship

Unigo Make Me Laugh Scholarship

ELIGIBLE APPLICANT: Grades 9-12

OTHER ELIGIBILITY: U.S. citizen or legal resident.

OVERVIEW: This is one of the many fun scholarships that are offered throughout the year by Unigo. Students create a free Unigo account and submit a short essay (up to 250 words) for the question "OMG... finding and applying for scholarships is serious business, but it's time to lighten things up a little. We don't want to know why you deserve $1,500 or how great your grades are. We simply want to LOL. Describe an incident in your life, funny or embarrassing (fact or fiction), and make us laugh!" Judges select the winner based on the essay.

AWARD: $1,500 for the winner.

DEADLINE: August 31, 2016

PROVIDER: Unigo

WEBSITE: www.unigo.com/scholarships/our-scholarships/make-me-laugh-scholarship

Unigo Shout It Out Scholarship

ELIGIBLE APPLICANT: Grades 9-12

OTHER ELIGIBILITY: U.S. citizen or legal resident.

OVERVIEW: This is one of the many fun scholarships that are offered throughout the year by Unigo. Students create a free Unigo account and submit a short essay (up to 250 words) for the question "If you could say one thing to the entire world at once, what would it be and why?" Judges select the winner based on the essay.

AWARD: $1,500 for the winner.

DEADLINE: September 30, 2016

PROVIDER: Unigo

WEBSITE: www.unigo.com/scholarships/our-scholarships/shout-it-out-scholarship

Unigo Superpower Scholarship

ELIGIBLE APPLICANT: Grades 9-12

OTHER ELIGIBILITY: U.S. citizen or legal resident.

OVERVIEW: This is one of the many fun scholarships that are offered throughout the year by Unigo. Students create a free Unigo account and submit a short essay (up to 250 words) for the question "Which superhero or villain would you want to change places with for a day and why?" Judges select the winner based on the essay.

AWARD: $2,500 for the winner.

DEADLINE: March 31, 2016

PROVIDER: Unigo

WEBSITE: www.unigo.com/scholarships/our-scholarships/ superpower-scholarship

Unigo Zombie Apocalypse Scholarship

ELIGIBLE APPLICANT: Grades 9-12

OTHER ELIGIBILITY: U.S. citizen or legal resident.

OVERVIEW: This is one of the many fun scholarships that are offered throughout the year by Unigo. Students create a free Unigo account and submit a short essay (up to 250 words) for the question "Imagine that your high school has been overrun with Zombies. Your math professor, the cafeteria ladies and even your best friend have all joined the walking dead. Use your brain to flesh out a plan to avoid the Zombies, including where you would hide and the top 5 things you would bring with you to stay alive." Judges select the winner based on the essay.

AWARD: $2,000 for the winner.

DEADLINE: October 31, 2016

PROVIDER: Unigo

WEBSITE: www.unigo.com/scholarships/our-scholarships/zombie-apocalypse-scholarship

U.S. Junior Chamber International (JCI) Senate Foundation Scholarship Program

ELIGIBLE APPLICANT: Seniors

OTHER ELIGIBILITY: U.S. citizen attending high school in the U.S. or an approved location. Applications must come from high school students from states that have a U.S. JCI Senate program.

OVERVIEW: The U.S. JCI Senate Foundation offers grants to students from states that have a U.S. JCI Senate program. Refer to the website for a list of eligible states. The two top applicants from each state are forwarded to the U.S. JCI Senate Foundation for scholarship consideration.

AWARD: $1,000. The number of awards varies.

DEADLINE: January

PROVIDER: U.S. JCI Senate Foundation

WEBSITE: www.usjcisenate.org/index.php/programs/scholarship

Voice of Democracy Contest

ELIGIBLE APPLICANT: Grades 9-12

OTHER ELIGIBILITY: Students attending high school in the U.S. who will attend college or trade/technical school in the U.S.

OVERVIEW: An annual contest for students to express themselves on democratic ideas and principles. The contest starts at the local level. Students write and record an essay on an audio CD or flash drive. They submit the typed essay and CD or flash drive to their local participating VFW Post. Refer to the website for VFW Post locations. There are various levels of competition and the state winner advances to the national level.

AWARD: $30,000 for the winner. Other national scholarships are provided in amounts of $1,000 to $16,000. The first place winner from each state receives a minimum scholarship of $1,000.

DEADLINE: November

PROVIDER: Veterans of Foreign Wars (VFW)

WEBSITE: www.vfw.org/Community/Voice-of-Democracy

We The Future Contest

ELIGIBLE APPLICANT: Grades 9-12

OTHER ELIGIBILITY: U.S. citizen or legal resident. Students attending school in the U.S., its territories or American Armed Forces School abroad.

OVERVIEW: Annual contests for students to promote and express themselves about the U.S. Constitution. There are six contest categories. Students may enter once per category. The six categories are entrepreneurial, petition/essay, public service announcement, short film, song and STEM. Refer to the website for contest information.

AWARD: $1,000 for the winner of each category.

DEADLINE: December

PROVIDER: Constituting America

WEBSITE: www.constitutingamerica.org/docs/WTPhs.pdf

We The Students Essay Contest

ELIGIBLE APPLICANT: Grades 9-12

OTHER ELIGIBILITY: U.S. citizen or legal resident. Students attending school in the U.S., its territories or American Armed Forces School abroad.

OVERVIEW: An annual essay (500-800 words) contest on the Declaration of Independence, the Constitution and the Bill of Rights. Judges evaluate submissions on adherence to essay guidelines, depth of the topic analysis, strength of the student's personal response, originality and writing style. Refer to the website for the annual essay prompt.

AWARD: $5,000 for the student winner along with a scholarship to Constitution Academy. $1,250 for 6 student runners up. $500 for 8 Student Honorable Mentions.

DEADLINE: Refer to the website for the next contest and deadline.

PROVIDER: Bill of Rights Institute

WEBSITE: http://billofrightsinstitute.org/engage/students-programs-events/scholarship

WyzAnt College Scholarship Contest

ELIGIBLE APPLICANT: Age 16 and up

OTHER ELIGIBILITY: U.S. citizen or legal resident who will enroll in a two-year or four-year college in the U.S. within the next two years.

OVERVIEW: Students write an essay (up to 300 words) about a person who inspired them. During the promotion period, all entries are displayed on the website for public voting. The ten entries with the highest number of public votes move on to the second round. In addition, judges select ten more entries for the second round. The twenty entries will then be judged by tutors who are registered and active on this website. Three winners will be selected based on expression of the question, creativity, and originality.

AWARD: $10,000 for 1st place, $3,000 for 2nd, $2,000 for 3rd place.

DEADLINE: May 1, 2016

PROVIDER: WyzAnt

WEBSITE: www.wyzant.com/scholarships

Young American Creative Patriotic Art Awards

ELIGIBLE APPLICANT: Grades 9-12

OTHER ELIGIBILITY: Students attending high school in the same state as the sponsoring VFW Auxiliary.

OVERVIEW: An annual art contest to show patriotism. Students submit one piece of patriotic art on canvas or paper. The artwork must be signed by a high school teacher and submitted to a local VFW Auxiliary. The first place winner from each local VFW Auxiliary will move on to the national competition. Students may contact the VFW National Headquarters to get connected with a local sponsoring post and/or Auxiliary.

AWARD: $10,000 for the winner, $5,000 for second place, $2,500 for third place, $1,500 for fourth place, $500 for fifth through eighth place.

DEADLINE: March

PROVIDER: Veterans of Foreign Wars (VFW) Auxiliary

WEBSITE: www.vfwauxiliary.org/programs-page/scholarships

Young Patriot Essay Contest

ELIGIBLE APPLICANT: Grades 9-12

OTHER ELIGIBILITY: U.S. citizen or legal resident.

OVERVIEW: An annual essay contest (no more than 1,200 words) on a controversial topic. For example, the 2015 topic was "Should the emerging and ongoing threat of global terrorism change how we view government surveillance as it relates to the 4th Amendment? Why or Why Not?" Judges will evaluate essays on writing skill, level of engagement with the topic and strength of reasoning. The award may be used for tuition or related expenses at any college. Refer to the website for the current topic.

AWARD: $5,000 for 1st place, $2,500 for 2nd, $1,500 for 3rd place.

DEADLINE: January

PROVIDER: National Center for Policy Analysis

WEBSITE: http://debate-central.ncpa.org/young_patriots_essay_contest_scholarship_1516

Youth Free Expression Network Film Contest

ELIGIBLE APPLICANT: Grades 9-12

OTHER ELIGIBILITY: Students living in the U.S. or its territories.

OVERVIEW: An annual program for students to express their thoughts on First Amendment rights and free speech. Students create a film (up to 4 minutes) in response to a topic posted on the website. The entries can be a documentary, animation, experimental, satire, fictional narrative or music video. The film entry must include a report that explains the intent of the film, the creative process and technical accomplishments.

AWARD: The winner receives an $1,000 award and a $5,000 scholarship for the New York Film Academy, $500 for second place, $250 for third place.

DEADLINE: December

PROVIDER: National Coalition Against Censorship (NCAC)

WEBSITE: http://ncac.org/project/film-contest

Chapter Three

National Scholarships/ Financial Need-Based

This chapter identifies national scholarships that have financial need as a component for eligibility. While there may be additional eligibility requirements, such as academic achievement or community service, financial need is a key factor.

It is important to note that scholarships do not utilize a standard definition for financial need. Some scholarships have a maximum household income amount or utilize the Federal Pell Grant eligibility criteria. Other scholarships do not have a clear definition for financial need. Instead, eligibility is determined on a case-by-case basis and requires a demonstrated financial need or evidence of a financial hardship.

The scholarships are listed in alphabetical order by scholarship name.

Courage to Grow Scholarship

ELIGIBLE APPLICANT: Grades 11-12

OTHER ELIGIBILITY: Financial Need. 2.5 GPA. U.S. citizen.

OVERVIEW: This monthly essay (up to 250 words) contest was created to help students with a financial need to pay for college. Applicants write about why they believe that they should be awarded this scholarship. The winner is selected based on the essay. Students may reapply every month.

AWARD: $500 for one winner every month.

DEADLINE: Monthly

PROVIDER: Courage to Grow

WEBSITE: www.couragetogrowscholarship.com

Dell Scholars Program

ELIGIBLE APPLICANT: Seniors

OTHER ELIGIBILITY: Financial Need (defined as meeting Federal Pell Grant eligibility). 2.4 GPA. Students who participated in a Michael & Susan Dell Foundation approved college readiness program in 11th and 12th grade. U.S. citizen or immigration residency status that qualifies for federal financial aid. Students intending to enroll full time in an accredited two-year or four-year college in the U.S. during Fall after high school graduation.

OVERVIEW: A prestigious annual financial need-based scholarship program to reach underserved students who are academically prepared for college. Students apply online after which a group of semi-finalists are selected. The Semi-finalists are required to submit additional documents, such as a high school transcript and letter of recommendation. Students are evaluated on determination to succeed, future goals and plans to achieve them, ability to communicate the hardships they face or overcome, self-motivation in completing challenging coursework and a demonstrated financial need. The Dell Scholars are subsequently selected. Refer to the website for additional information.

AWARD: $20,000, and a laptop and textbook credits to 300 recipients.

DEADLINE: January

PROVIDER: Michael & Susan Dell Foundation

WEBSITE: www.dellscholars.org

Elks National Foundation Most Valuable Student Competition

ELIGIBLE APPLICANT: Seniors

OTHER ELIGIBILITY: Financial Need. U.S. citizen. Taken SAT or ACT by November. Students enrolling in a four-year U.S. college.

OVERVIEW: A financial need-based scholarship program sponsored by the Elks. Students apply by submitting an application to the Elks Lodge closest to the student's permanent U.S. residence. Refer to the website for Elk Lodge locations. Applicants must advance through local, district and state competitions to reach the national competition. Judges select scholarship recipients based on leadership and financial need. Male and female students compete separately. Applicants are not required to be related to a member of the Elks.

AWARD: $12,500 renewable annually ($50,000 total) for 2 first place winners. $10,000 renewable annually ($40,000 total) for 2 second place winners. $7,500 renewable annually ($30,000 total) for 4 years for 2 third place winners. $5,000 renewable annually ($20,000 total) for 2 forth place winners. $1,000 renewable annually ($4,000 total) for 480 runners up.

NOTE: Local, district and state Elks lodges and associations may award its own scholarships.

DEADLINE: December

PROVIDER: Elks National Foundation

WEBSITE: www.elks.org/ENF/scholars/mvs.cfm

Engebretson Foundation Scholarship

ELIGIBLE APPLICANT: Seniors

OTHER ELIGIBILITY: Financial Need. 3.75 GPA or top 5% rank in the high school class. 28 ACT or 1240 SAT.

OVERVIEW: The scholarship is awarded to students with exceptional academic and leadership ability and potential. The application includes an essay (up to 750 words). The scholarship may be used at any accredited four-year college approved by the Foundation. Judges will consider financial need, academic achievements, teacher recommendation, work experience, extra-curricular activities and community service.

AWARD: $5,000 per semester renewable ($40,000 total) for 1 winner.

DEADLINE: March

PROVIDER: Engebretson Foundation

WEBSITE: www.engebretsonfoundation.org

Ge-Reagan Foundation Scholarship Program

ELIGIBLE APPLICANT: Seniors

OTHER ELIGIBILITY: Financial Need. 3.0 GPA. US. citizen. Students attending high school in the U.S. who will attend an accredited four-year college in the U.S in the Fall after high school graduation on a full-time basis.

OVERVIEW: A scholarship program for students who excel academically and in areas of leadership, drive, integrity and citizenship. Students must be nominated by a high school principal, elected official, executive director of a non-profit organization of other eligible community leader. Students are required to demonstrate financial need

AWARD: $10,000 renewable annually ($40,000 total). Approximately 20 awards are provided.

DEADLINE: Refer to website for the next application cycle.

PROVIDER: Ronald Reagan Presidential Foundation & Library

WEBSITE: www.reaganfoundation.org/GE-RFScholarships.aspx

Haden Scholarships

ELIGIBLE APPLICANT: Seniors

OTHER ELIGIBILITY: Financial Need. 3.5 GPA. U.S. citizens.

OVERVIEW: An annual scholarship program to provide exceptional students with financial aid. Students submit their ACT/SAT scores, transcript, class ranking, financial statements, an essay, two letters of recommendation, their first and second college choices and intended course of study. Applicants are evaluated on academics, character, financial need, extra-curricular activities and community service.

AWARD: $2,500 to $4,000 renewable annually ($10,000 to $16,000 total). The number of awards varies.

DEADLINE: February.

PROVIDER: Youth Foundation

WEBSITE: http://fdnweb.org/youthfdn

Horatio Alger National Scholarships

ELIGIBLE APPLICANT: Seniors

OTHER ELIGIBILITY: Financial Need ($55,000 or less adjusted gross family income). 2.0 GPA. Students who overcame significant adversity. U.S. citizens who will attend an accredited not-for-profit college in the U.S. on a full-time basis. Idaho, Louisiana and Montana residents must attend a specific college in their respective state.

OVERVIEW: A scholarship program to provide financial aid to students who faced and overcame great obstacles in their lives. The application form requires a detailed description and verification of the adversity. Students must be involved in school and community service activities.

AWARD: $22,000 for 106 recipients.

DEADLINE: Refer to website for next application cycle.

PROVIDER: Horatio Alger Association of Distinguished Americans

WEBSITE: https://scholars.horatioalger.org/scholarships/about-our-scholarship-programs

Imagine America High School Scholarship

ELIGIBLE APPLICANT: Seniors

OTHER ELIGIBILITY: Financial need. 2.5 GPA.

OVERVIEW: An annual program to assist students with financial need to pursue an education at one of 550 participating "career" colleges. Students must be nominated by their school and demonstrate voluntary community service during their senior year. Refer to the website for a list of participating career colleges.

AWARD: $1,000. The number of awards varies.

DEADLINE: December

PROVIDER: Imagine America Foundation

WEBSITE: www.imagine-america.org/faq/imagine-america-high-school-scholarships

Jack Kent Cooke Foundation College Scholarship

ELIGIBLE APPLICANT: Seniors

OTHER ELIGIBILITY: Financial Need (generally meeting Federal Pell Grant eligibility, but family income up to $95,000 is considered). 3.5 GPA. Top 15% nationally on SAT/ACT. A minimum of 26 on ACT or 1,200 on SAT. U.S. students intending to enroll full time in an accredited four-year college.

OVERVIEW: An annual financial need-based scholarship program to assist high-achieving students who seek to attend and graduate from the best four-year colleges. Students undergo a rigorous application process and are evaluated on academic excellence, persistence, leadership, community service, demonstrated financial need and other criteria.

AWARD: Up to $40,000 renewable annually. The number of awards varies, but typically 30-40 recipients.

DEADLINE: Refer to the website for the next application cycle.

PROVIDER: Jack Kent Cooke Foundation

WEBSITE: www.jkcf.org/scholarship-programs/college-scholarship

Nordstrom Scholarship

ELIGIBLE APPLICANT: Juniors

OTHER ELIGIBILITY: Financial Need. 2.7 GPA. US. citizen. Students attending high school in a participating state designated by Nordstrom. Students who plan to attend an accredited four-year college in the U.S.

OVERVIEW: Nordstrom has an annual scholarship program. Students are evaluated on financial need, academic achievement, community service, leadership, employment, honors, awards and other criteria. Semifinalists require a recommendation from a high school official.

AWARD: $2,500 renewable annually ($10,000 total). Approximately 20 awards are provided.

DEADLINE: Refer to website for the next application cycle.

PROVIDER: Nordstrom

WEBSITE: www.nordstrom.scholarsapply.org

Ronald McDonald House Charities/ Scholars – U.S. Scholarships

ELIGIBLE APPLICANT: Seniors

OTHER ELIGIBILITY: Financial Need. 2.7 GPA. U.S. citizens or legal residents enrolling full-time in a two-year or four-year college or technical school. Students living in a participating RMHC areas.

OVERVIEW: A scholarship program for students from communities who have limited access to educational and career opportunities. Students must demonstrate community service, academic achievement and leadership. Refer to the website for participating RMHC areas.

AWARD: Typically at least $1,000. The number of awards varies.

DEADLINE: Refer to the website for the next application cycle.

PROVIDER: Ronald McDonald House Charities

WEBSITE: www.rmhc.org/rmhc-us-scholarships

State Farm Good Neighbor Scholarship

ELIGIBLE APPLICANT: Seniors

OTHER ELIGIBILITY: Financial Need. 2.5 to 3.2 GPA. US. citizen. Students who plan to enroll in an accredited two-year or four-year college or technical/vocational upon graduating from high school on a full-time basis.

OVERVIEW: State Farm has an annual scholarship program. Students are evaluated on financial need, community service, leadership and other criteria.

AWARD: $2,500. The number of awards varies.

DEADLINE: Refer to website for the next application cycle.

PROVIDER: State Farm

WEBSITE: www.scholarshipamerica.org/statefarmgoodneighbor scholarship

Chapter Four

National Scholarships/ Nationality, Race & Ethnic Heritage

This chapter contains national scholarships that are intended for students of a specific nationality, race or ethnic heritage. Typically, partial heritage is considered a qualifier, but some scholarships allow for one quarter heritage.

The scholarships are listed in alphabetical order by scholarship name.

Congressional Black Caucus (CBC) Scholarships

ELIGIBLE APPLICANT: Seniors

OTHER ELIGIBILITY: Students who live in a district represented by a member of the CBC. U.S. citizen or permanent legal resident.

OVERVIEW: The CBC offers scholarships to students who demonstrate leadership through community service and academic achievement. In addition, scholarships are offered to students with a demonstrated financial need to reward their persistence in pursuing an education. Refer to the website for available scholarships.

AWARD: The amount varies by scholarship. Over 200 awards are provided annually.

DEADLINE: Refer to the website for the application cycles of the scholarships.

PROVIDER: Congressional Black Caucus

WEBSITE: www.cbcfinc.org/scholarships

Congressional Hispanic Caucus Institute (CHCI) Scholarships

ELIGIBLE APPLICANT: Seniors

OTHER ELIGIBILITY: Financial Need. U.S. citizens, legal permanent residents, asylees, or individuals who are lawfully authorized to work without restriction for any U.S. employer. Students planning to enroll full-time in an accredited two-year or four-year college.

OVERVIEW: The CHCI offers scholarships to students who demonstrate leadership and community service. Refer to the website for additional information.

AWARD: $1,000 for an Associate's Degree. $2,500 for a Bachelor's Degree. The number of awards varies.

DEADLINE: Refer to the website for the application cycle.

PROVIDER: Congressional Hispanic Caucus Institute

WEBSITE: www.chci.org/programs/scholarships

Denny's Hungry for Education Scholarship/ U.S. Hispanic Leadership Institute (USHLI)

ELIGIBLE APPLICANT: Grades 9-12

OTHER ELIGIBILITY: Refer to the website for information.

OVERVIEW: Denny's and the U.S. Hispanic Leadership Institute (USHLI) have partnered to offer this scholarship. Applicants must apply through the Denny's scholarship website.

AWARD: $3,000 for the winner. Awards are provided to 3 recipients.

DEADLINE: Refer to the website for the next application cycle.

PROVIDER: Denny's & U.S. Hispanic Leadership Institute

WEBSITE: https://dennysscholarships.versaic.com/login

Denny's Hungry for Education Scholarship/ U.S. Pan Asian American Chamber of Commerce

ELIGIBLE APPLICANT: Grades 9-12

OTHER ELIGIBILITY: Asian-Pacific Island heritage. 2.5 GPA. Students living in the U.S.

OVERVIEW: Denny's partnered with the U.S. Pan Asian American Chamber of Commerce Education Foundation to offer this scholarship. The application requires an essay (up to 300 words) on the topic "How Denny's can impact childhood hunger in their local communities?" Applicants must apply through the Denny's scholarship website.

AWARD: $3,000 for the winner.

DEADLINE: March 25, 2016

PROVIDER: Denny's & U.S. Pan Asian American Chamber of Commerce Education Foundation

WEBSITE: https://dennysscholarships.versaic.com/login

Gates Millennium Scholars/African American

ELIGIBLE APPLICANT: Seniors

OTHER ELIGIBILITY: African American. Financial Need (defined as meeting Federal Pell Grant eligibility). 3.3 GPA. U.S. citizen, legal permanent resident or national. Students enrolling full time in a U.S. accredited college.

OVERVIEW: An annual scholarship program to promote academic excellence and provide opportunities for minority students with significant financial need. Students must demonstrate leadership abilities through participation in school activities, community service and other activities. Students must be nominated by a principal, guidance counselor or teacher.

AWARD: The amount and number of awards varies.

DEADLINE: Refer to the website for the next application cycle.

PROVIDER: Bill & Melinda Gates Foundation.

WEBSITE: www.gmsp.org/publicweb/aboutus.aspx

Gates Millennium Scholars/ American Indian-Alaska Native

ELIGIBLE APPLICANT: Seniors

OTHER ELIGIBILITY: American Indian/Alaska Native. Financial Need (defined as meeting Federal Pell Grant eligibility). 3.3 GPA. U.S. citizen, legal permanent resident or national.

OVERVIEW: An annual program to promote academic excellence and provide opportunities for minority students with significant financial need. Students must demonstrate leadership through participation in school and community service activities. Students must be nominated by an educator.

AWARD: The amount and number of awards varies.

DEADLINE: Refer to the website for the next application cycle.

PROVIDER: Bill & Melinda Gates Foundation.

WEBSITE: www.gmsp.org/publicweb/aboutus.aspx

Gates Millennium Scholars/ Asian American-Pacific Islander

ELIGIBLE APPLICANT: Seniors

OTHER ELIGIBILITY: Asian American/Pacific Islander. Financial Need (defined as meeting Federal Pell Grant eligibility). 3.3 GPA. U.S. citizen, legal resident or national. Students enrolling full time in a U.S. accredited college.

OVERVIEW: An annual program to promote academic excellence and provide opportunities for minority students with significant financial need. Students must demonstrate leadership through participation in school and community service activities. Students must be nominated by an educator.

AWARD: The amount and number of awards varies.

DEADLINE: Refer to the website for the next application cycle.

PROVIDER: Bill & Melinda Gates Foundation.

WEBSITE: www.gmsp.org/publicweb/aboutus.aspx

Gates Millennium Scholars/Hispanic American

ELIGIBLE APPLICANT: Seniors

OTHER ELIGIBILITY: Hispanic American. Financial Need (defined as meeting Federal Pell Grant eligibility). 3.3 GPA. U.S. citizen, legal resident or national. Students enrolling full time in a U.S. accredited college.

OVERVIEW: An annual scholarship program to promote academic excellence and provide opportunities for minority students with significant financial need. Students must demonstrate leadership through participation in school and community service activities. Students must be nominated by an educator.

AWARD: The amount and number of awards varies.

DEADLINE: Refer to the website for the next application cycle.

PROVIDER: Bill & Melinda Gates Foundation.

WEBSITE: www.gmsp.org/publicweb/aboutus.aspx

Girl Friends Fund Scholarship

ELIGIBLE APPLICANT: Seniors

OTHER ELIGIBILITY: African-American. Financial Need. 3.0 GPA. 18 ACT or 1200 SAT. U.S. citizens accepted to a four-year accredited college.

OVERVIEW: To assist high-achieving male and female African-American students who face significant financial obstacles pursue a college education. Students apply to their local chapter of The Girl Friends, Inc. Each of the 47 chapters may nominate one student for scholarship consideration. Students may email the national organization for local chapter contact information.

AWARD: $1,000 to $1,500 renewable for four years ($4,000 to $6,000 total). The number of awards varies.

DEADLINE: March

PROVIDER: The Girl Friends Fund, Inc.

WEBSITE: www.imagine-america.org/faq/imagine-america-high-school-scholarships

Hispanic Scholarship Fund (HSF) Scholarships

ELIGIBLE APPLICANT: Seniors

OTHER ELIGIBILITY: Hispanic/Latino heritage. 3.0 GPA. U.S. citizen or permanent legal resident or DACA or Eligible Non-Citizen (as defined by FAFSA). Students enrolling full-time in an accredited four-year college in the U.S.

OVERVIEW: An annual scholarship fund to provide assistance to Hispanic/Latino students to further their education. Financial need is not an eligibility requirement, but may be used to determine the award amount.

AWARD: $500 to $5,000. The number of awards varies.

DEADLINE: March

PROVIDER: Hispanic Scholarship Fund

WEBSITE: www.hsf.net/en/scholarships

Jackie Robinson Foundation Scholar

ELIGIBLE APPLICANT: Seniors

OTHER ELIGIBILITY: Minority as defined by U.S. Census Bureau. Financial Need. 21 ACT or 1000 SAT. US. citizens. Students attending high school in the U.S. who will attend an accredited four-year college in the U.S.

OVERVIEW: A scholarship program for minority students who show leadership potential, community service involvement and a demonstrated financial need. Students apply online and submit a letter of recommendation. Financial need will be determined on a case-by-case basis. There is no formula.

AWARD: Up to $28,000. The number of awards varies.

DEADLINE: Refer to the website for the next application cycle.

PROVIDER: Jackie Robinson Foundation

WEBSITE: www.jackierobinson.org/apply/application-faqs

League of United Latin American Citizens (LULAC) National Scholarship

ELIGIBLE APPLICANT: Seniors

OTHER ELIGIBILITY: Students from a participating LULAC council state. Financial Need.

OVERVIEW: The LULAC Scholarship Fund helps youth in underserved communities attend college. There are three levels of scholarships. The National Scholastic Achievement requires a 3.5GPA and 29 on ACT or 1,350 on SAT. The Honors level requires a 3.0 GPA and 23 on ACT or 1,100 on SAT. The General level focuses on the student's motivation, sincerity, and community involvement. Refer to the website for participating states.

AWARD: $2,000 National Scholastic Achievement Award. $500 to $2,000 Honors Award. $250 to $500 General Award. The number of awards varies.

DEADLINE: Usually in March.

PROVIDER: LULAC National Scholarship Fund (LNSF)

WEBSITE: www.lnesc.org/#!lnsf/c17bl

Ronald McDonald House Charities/Asia – U.S.

ELIGIBLE APPLICANT: Seniors

OTHER ELIGIBILITY: Asian-Pacific heritage. 2.7 GPA. Financial Need. U.S. citizen or legal resident. Students enrolling full-time in a college or technical school. Students in a participating RMHC chapter geographic area.

OVERVIEW: Scholarships are provided to students from communities who face limited access to educational and career opportunities. Students must demonstrate community service, academic achievement and leadership. Refer to the website for participating areas.

AWARD: $1,000 or more. The number of awards varies.

DEADLINE: Refer to the website for the next application cycle.

PROVIDER: Ronald McDonald House Charities

WEBSITE: www.rmhc.org/rmhc-us-scholarships

Ronald McDonald House Charities/ African American Future Achievers – U.S.

ELIGIBLE APPLICANT: Seniors

OTHER ELIGIBILITY: African American or Black Caribbean heritage. 2.7 GPA. Financial Need. U.S. citizen or legal resident enrolling full-time in a two-year or four-year college or technical school. Students living in a participating RMHC Chapter's geographic area.

OVERVIEW: Scholarships are provided to students from communities who face limited access to educational and career opportunities. Students must demonstrate community service, academic achievement and leadership. Refer to the website for participating areas.

AWARD: $1,000 or more. The number of awards varies.

DEADLINE: Refer to the website for the next application cycle.

PROVIDER: Ronald McDonald House Charities

WEBSITE: www.rmhc.org/rmhc-us-scholarships

Ronald McDonald House Charities/HACAR – U.S.

ELIGIBLE APPLICANT: Seniors

OTHER ELIGIBILITY: Hispanic or Latino heritage. 2.7 GPA. Financial Need. U.S. citizen or legal resident enrolling full-time in a two-year or four-year college or technical school. Students living in a participating RMHC Chapter's geographic area

OVERVIEW: Scholarships are provided to students from communities who face limited access to educational and career opportunities. Students must demonstrate community service, academic achievement and leadership. Refer to the website for participating areas.

AWARD: $1,000 or more. The number of awards varies.

DEADLINE: Refer to the website for the next application cycle.

PROVIDER: Ronald McDonald House Charities

WEBSITE: www.rmhc.org/rmhc-us-scholarships

Ron Brown Scholarship

ELIGIBLE APPLICANT: Seniors

OTHER ELIGIBILITY: Black/African American heritage. Financial Need. U.S. citizen or permanent legal resident enrolling full-time in an accredited four-year college in the U.S.

OVERVIEW: This selective scholarship program is intended for economically challenged African Americans who excel academically and in the community. Students must demonstrate a great interest in public service, community engagement, business entrepreneurship and global citizenship. The application includes two essays of 500 words each.

AWARD: $10,000 renewable annually ($40,000 total). The number of awards varies.

DEADLINE: Currently November 1 for early applicant and January 9 for the normal deadline.

PROVIDER: Ron Brown Scholar Fund

WEBSITE: www.ronbrown.org/section/apply/program-description

Chapter Five

National Scholarships/ Religious Affiliation

This chapter contains national scholarships for students that identify with a specific religious faith. There may be additional eligibility requirements, such as financial need and/or academic achievement.

The scholarships are listed in alphabetical order by scholarship name.

American Baptist Home Mission Societies Undergraduate Scholarship

ELIGIBLE APPLICANT: Seniors

OTHER ELIGIBILITY: American Baptist Church member. Financial Need. U.S. citizen or permanent resident. Students enrolling full-time in an accredited college in the U.S. or Puerto Rico during Fall after high school graduation.

OVERVIEW: An annual scholarship program to provide financial aid to students who have been active members of an American Baptist Church for at least 12 months before applying.

AWARD: Varies. The scholarships are renewable.

DEADLINE: May

PROVIDER: American Baptist Home Mission Societies

WEBSITE: www.nationalministries.org/education/financial_aid/student_info.cfm

Diller Teen Tikkun Olam Award

ELIGIBLE APPLICANT: Grades 9-12

OTHER ELIGIBILITY: Jewish teenagers. U.S. resident.

OVERVIEW: Tikkun Olam (i.e., repair the world) is an annual awards program to acknowledge and celebrate Jewish teenagers who volunteer for community service and demonstrate leadership with their community service project. The project can involve the Jewish community or the general community. The teenagers may be nominated by an unrelated community member or they can nominate themselves. The award may be used for education or to further the teenager's community service project.

AWARD: $36,000. Awards are provided for up to 15 recipients.

DEADLINE: Refer to the website for the next application cycle.

PROVIDER: Helen Diller Family Foundation

WEBSITE: www.dillerteenawards.org

Dr. Abdulmunim A. Shakir Scholarship

ELIGIBLE APPLICANT: Seniors

OTHER ELIGIBILITY: Committed to Islam. 3.0 GPA. U.S. citizen.

OVERVIEW: An annual scholarship program for students committed to Islam. Students are evaluated on academics, leadership and community service.

AWARD: $1,000. 20 awards are provided.

DEADLINE: March. Refer to the website for the next application cycle.

PROVIDER: Abdulmunim Shakir Charitable Trust

WEBSITE: www.isna.net/shakir-scholarship.html

Kaplun Essay Contest

EIGIBLE APPLICANT: Grades 9-12

OTHER ELIGIBILITY: Jewish. Open to all other faiths. Students from anywhere in the world.

OVERVIEW: This foundation sponsors an annual essay contest to encourage young people to treasure Jewish heritage and values and gain a better understanding of Jewish contributions to civilization and culture. The contest is open to students of all faiths. Students compete in one of two levels depending on their grade. Level I is for grades 7-9 and Level II is for grades 10-12. The previous Level II essay prompt was "In View of the Fact that There is Anti-Semitism and Intolerance on So Many College Campuses Today, What Steps Will You Take (When You Get There) to Combat it?" Refer to the website for the current Level I and Level II essay prompt.

AWARD: $1,800 for the winner. $750 for 5 finalists. Awards are provided for each Level.

DEADLINE: March. Refer to the website for the next contest.

PROVIDER: The Morris J. & Betty Kaplun Foundation

WEBSITE: www.kaplunfoundation.org

Knights of Columbus Scholarships for Catholics

ELIGIBLE APPLICANT: Seniors

OTHER ELIGIBILITY: Children of a member of Knights of Columbus. Students enrolling in a Catholic college.

OVERVIEW: The Knights of Columbus provides scholarships primarily to members and children of members who enroll in a Catholic college. There are various scholarships. Refer to the website for additional information.

AWARD: Varies.

DEADLINE: Refer to the website for information.

PROVIDER: Knights of Columbus

WEBSITE: www.kofc.org/un/en/scholarships/index.html

National Presbyterian College Scholarships

ELIGIBLE APPLICANT: Seniors

OTHER ELIGIBILITY: Active member of the Presbyterian Church USA. 2.5 GPA. Financial Need. Students enrolling at a college related to the Presbyterian Church USA.

OVERVIEW: This annual scholarship program provides assistance to students who are members of the Presbyterian Church USA who will be attending a Presbyterian related college. There is a financial need component. Students must be endorsed by a church pastor or clerk.

AWARD: Up to $1,500. 25-30 awards are provided.

DEADLINE: Typically March.

PROVIDER: Presbyterian Church USA

WEBSITE: www.presbyterianmission.org/ministries/financialaid/national-presbyterian-college-scholarship

Play With Purpose Scholarship

ELIGIBLE APPLICANT: Grades 10-12

OTHER ELIGIBILITY: Devote Christian. 2.0 GPA. Athlete on a Varsity team.

OVERVIEW: This annual program provides scholarships to recognize devote Christian student athletes who participate on one or more varsity-level high school team in one of 33 sanctioned sports. The student athlete must be nominated by the school, coach, youth pastor, parent or other person.

AWARD: $2,000 for 4 winners. Awards are provided for an additional 20 student athletes.

DEADLINE: February

PROVIDER: SportQuest Ministries, Inc.

WEBSITE: www.allamericanaward.org/criteria.html

Simmons & Fletcher Christian Studies Scholarship

ELIGIBLE APPLICANT: Seniors

OTHER ELIGIBILITY: Students enrolling at a Christian college. 3.0 GPA. U.S. citizen or permanent resident.

OVERVIEW: This program provides scholarships to students attending a Christian college. Students submit an essay (up to 1,000 words) about how a Christian education and Christian business leaders help to enhance the moral fibers of the U.S. and how a Christian education will benefit them.

AWARD: $1,000 for the winner. $500 for the runner-up.

DEADLINE: October 15, 2016

PROVIDER: Simmons & Fletcher, P.C.

WEBSITE: www.simmonsandfletcher.com/christian-studies-scholarship

United Methodist Higher Education Foundation Scholarship

ELIGIBLE APPLICANT: Seniors

OTHER ELIGIBILITY: Active member of the United Methodist Church. Students enrolling at a college related to the United Methodist Church.

OVERVIEW: The UMHEF has many types of scholarships for students who are active, full members of the United Methodist Church for at least one year who will enroll at a college related to the United Methodist Church. Other Methodist denominations are not eligible for a scholarship. Refer to the website for information.

AWARD: Varies

DEADLINE: Typically March

PROVIDER: United Methodist Higher Education Foundation (UMHEF)

WEBSITE: www.umhef.org/faq-category/scholarship-awards

Chapter Six

National Scholarships/ Degree or Career Interest

There are many scholarships based on a student's degree or career interest. A majority of these scholarships are intended for students that are already attending college and are taking courses towards a specific career or have declared a major. This chapter identifies scholarships based on degree or career interest for which high school students are eligible to apply.

The scholarships are listed in alphabetical order by scholarship name.

Buick Achievers Scholarship Program

ELIGIBLE APPLICANT: Seniors

OTHER ELIGIBILITY: Students intending to major in engineering, technology or select design and business related program. U.S. citizens. Students attending an accredited 4 year college in the U.S. or Puerto Rico.

OVERVIEW: Students are evaluated on their academics, participation and leadership in community and school activities, demonstrated financial need, work experience and interest in pursuing a career in the automotive or related industries. Other considerations may include female, minority, first-generation college student and dependent of military personnel.

AWARD: Up to $25,000 per year renewable for up to four years, and one additional year for a qualifying five-year engineering program. The award is provided to 50 recipients.

DEADLINE: Refer to the website for the next application cycle.

PROVIDER: The GM Foundation

WEBSITE: www.buickachievers.com

Central Intelligence Agency (CIA) Undergraduate Scholarship Program

ELIGIBLE APPLICANT: Seniors (age 18 by April 1st)

OTHER ELIGIBILITY: Work summers for the CIA. Financial Need (defined as up to $70,000 in income for family of four and $80,000 for family for five). 3.0 GPA. Minimum 21 on ACT or 1500 SAT (1000 Math & Critical Reading/500 Writing). U.S. citizens who will attend a 4 year college.

OVERVIEW: This competitive scholarship program offers students career experience with the CIA. The program requires summer work for the CIA in Washington D.C. Students are given work that is relevant to their chosen major or skill set. Financial need is one of the application requirements. Refer to the website for additional information.

AWARD: Up to $18,000 for college renewable annually. In addition, students receive an employment package consisting of salary and benefits. The number of awards varies.

DEADLINE: Refer to the website for the next application cycle.

PROVIDER: Central Intelligence Agency (CIA)

WEBSITE: www.cia.gov/careers/student-opportunities/undergraduate-scholarship-program.html

David S. Barr Award for Student Journalism

ELIGIBLE APPLICANT: Grades 9-12

OTHER ELIGIBILITY: Involvement in journalism

OVERVIEW: An annual award program for aspiring journalists. Students submit one entry along with a summary of their work. The application must be signed by a teacher.

AWARD: $1,000 for the winner.

DEADLINE: January

PROVIDER: The Newspaper Guild, Communications Workers of America

WEBSITE: www.newsguild.org/david-s-barr-award-student-journalism

Intel Science Talent Search

ELIGIBLE APPLICANT: Seniors

OTHER ELIGIBILITY: U.S. citizens.

OVERVIEW: An annual science competition to honor exceptional students for their scientific research and potential as future leaders in the scientific community. Judges select 300 semifinalists then 40 finalists. The finalists are invited to Washington, D.C. to compete in three categories of Basic Research, Global Good and Innovation.

AWARD: $150,000 for 3 first place winners. $750,000 for 3 second place winners. $35,000 for 3 third place winners. $7,500 for the remaining 31 finalists. Awards are also provided to semifinalists.

DEADLINE: Refer to the website for the next contest cycle.

PROVIDER: Intel

WEBSITE: www.intel.com/content/www/us/en/education/competitions/science-talent-search.html

Intertech Foundation STM Scholarship

ELIGIBLE APPLICANT: Seniors

OTHER ELIGIBILITY: Students intending to major in Computer Science. 3.3 GPA. U.S. citizens who will attend an accredited U.S. college.

OVERVIEW: An annual scholarship program to support students interested in pursuing a career as software developers. Students submit their transcript, a copy of a college acceptance letter when available, two letters of recommendation and an essay about how they plan to participate in the professional software development industry. Applicants will be evaluated on grade point average, ACT/SAT, participation in extracurricular activities, elected leadership positions, community service, references and the essay.

AWARD: $2,500 for the winner.

DEADLINE: March

PROVIDER: Intertech Consulting

WEBSITE: www.intertech.com/About/Foundation/Scholarship

National Security Agency (NSA) Stokes Educational Scholarship Program

ELIGIBLE APPLICANT: Seniors

OTHER ELIGIBILITY: Work summers for the NSA. 3.0 GPA. Minimum 25 on ACT or 1600 SAT (1100 Math & Critical Reading/500 Writing). U.S. citizens who will attend a four-year college and plan to major in computer science or computer/electrical engineering.

OVERVIEW: This competitive scholarship program offers students career experience with the NSA and facilitates the recruitment of students who plan to major in computer science or computer/electrical engineering, particularly minorities. The program requires summer work for the NSA.

AWARD: Up to $30,000 for college renewable annually. In addition, students receive an employment package consisting of salary and benefits. The number of awards varies.

DEADLINE: Refer to the website for the next application cycle.

PROVIDER: National Security Agency (NSA)

WEBSITE: www.intelligencecareers.gov/icstudents.html? Agency=NSA

Neuroscience Research Prize

ELIGIBLE APPLICANT: Grades 9-12

OTHER ELIGIBILITY: Neuroscience research. Students in the U.S.

OVERVIEW: An annual award to students who show potential for scientific contributions in the field of neuroscience. Students submit original laboratory research and written work related to the brain or nervous system. Group projects are not eligible.

AWARD: $1,000 for 4 winners. Additional awards for 3 of those winners.

DEADLINE: Refer to the website for the next deadline.

PROVIDER: American Academy of Neurology

WEBSITE: http://tools.aan.com/science/awards/?fuseaction=home.info&id=11

Reserve Officer Training Corps (ROTC) Scholarships

ELIGIBLE APPLICANT: Seniors

OTHER ELIGIBILITY: Commitment to the military for the specified number of years. Minimum GPA and ACT/SAT as specified by the military armed service branch. Physical fitness assessment. Attend a college having an ROTC program.

OVERVIEW: The U.S. military offers college scholarships and monthly pay for students interested in becoming an officer in exchange for those students serving as an officer for a specified amount of time upon graduating from college. ROTC units are located on college campuses and provide military training for a few hours each week. Students may apply to an ROTC program for the Army, Airforce and Navy. In addition, students interested in the Marine Corps can participate in the Navy ROTC program. Students may be required to major in a specific area if awarded an ROTC scholarship. Refer to the applicable website and recruitment office or additional information.

AWARD: Varies. Approximately 4,000 recipients are selected annually between the various military armed services branches.

DEADLINE: Refer to the website and recruitment office for the application cycle.

ARMY WEBSITE: www.goarmy.com/rotc/high-school-students/ four-year-scholarship.html

AIRFORCE WEBSITE: www.afrotc.com/scholarships

NAVY WEBSITE: www.nrotc.navy.mil/scholarship_criteria.aspx

SanDisk Scholars Program

ELIGIBLE APPLICANT: Seniors

OTHER ELIGIBILITY: Students intending to major in Computer Science and Engineering or related field. 3.0 GPA. Financial Need. U.S. citizen or legal resident who will attend an accredited U.S. college in the Fall following high school graduation on a full-time basis.

OVERVIEW: An annual scholars program to support the educational goals of students in pursuit of careers in engineering and computer science. Students will be evaluated on financial need, community involvement, leadership and/or entrepreneurial interests, their essay and academics.

AWARD: $2,500 renewable annually ($10,000 in total). The number of awards varies.

DEADLINE: Refer to the website for the next application cycle.

PROVIDER: SanDisk

WEBSITE: www.sandisk.com/about/corp-responsibility/scholars-program

Society of Automotive Engineers (SAE) International Scholarship Program

ELIGIBLE APPLICANT: Seniors

OTHER ELIGIBILITY: Students intending to major in engineering or related field. U.S. residents. GPA, ACT/SAT and other criteria.

OVERVIEW: SAE International has many scholarships available to students intending to major in engineering or related field. Refer to the website for the scholarships and the eligibility and application requirements. There are currently eight scholarships for high school seniors.

AWARD: Refer to the specific scholarship.

DEADLINE: Refer to each scholarship for its application deadline.

PROVIDER: SAE International

WEBSITE: http://students.sae.org/scholarships/freshman

The National Press Club Scholarship for Journalism Diversity

ELIGIBLE APPLICANT: Seniors

OTHER ELIGIBILITY: Students intending to major in Journalism. 3.0 GPA. Students accepted into an accredited four-year college.

OVERVIEW: An annual scholarship program for students interested in pursuing a career in journalism who will bring diversity to the field. Students submit an application along with other documents including up to five work samples and an essay. The essay (500 words) should explain how the student will add diversity to U.S. journalism.

AWARD: $2,500 renewable annually ($10,000 total) for the winner.

DEADLINE: March

PROVIDER: National Press Club

WEBSITE: www.press.org/about/scholarships/diversity

The Richard G. Zimmerman Journalism Scholarship

ELIGIBLE APPLICANT: Seniors

OTHER ELIGIBILITY: Students intending to major in Journalism. 3.0 GPA. Students accepted into an accredited four-year college.

OVERVIEW: An annual scholarship program for students interested in pursuing a career in journalism. Students submit an application along with other documents including three work samples.

AWARD: $5,000 for the winner.

DEADLINE: March

PROVIDER: National Press Club

WEBSITE: www.press.org/about/scholarships/zimmerman

Toshiba Machine Company America Scholarship

ELIGIBLE APPLICANT: Seniors

OTHER ELIGIBILITY: Students intending to major in an industrial maintenance or plastic processing related program. 3.0 GPA. Students planning to enroll in an accredited two-year or four-year college or vocational/technical school in the Fall upon high school graduation.

OVERVIEW: An annual scholarship program for students interested in pursuing an industrial maintenance or plastic processing program of study. Judges consider a student's academic achievement, involvement in community service, statement of goals and aspirations, and other categories.

AWARD: $2,500. Up to two awards are provided.

DEADLINE: February

PROVIDER: Toshiba Machine Company, America

WEBSITE: www.toshiba-machine.com/Upload/Product/TMA%20Scholarship%20Guidelines%20and%20Application1.pdf

Tuskegee Airmen Scholarship

ELIGIBLE APPLICANT: Seniors

OTHER ELIGIBILITY: Students interested in aviation, aerospace engineering or related field. 3.0 GPA. Financial Need.

OVERVIEW: An annual program to preserve the legacy of the Tuskegee Airmen and provide scholarships to financially disadvantaged students interested in aviation, aerospace engineering or related field. The application includes an essay on the Tuskegee Airmen and an essay about the student. Judges consider a student's academic achievement, involvement in extracurricular activities, character and financial need.

AWARD: $1,500 to 40 recipients.

DEADLINE: February

PROVIDER: Tuskegee Airmen Scholarship Foundation

WEBSITE: www.taisf.org

U.S. Senate Youth Program Scholarship

ELIGIBLE APPLICANT: Grades 11-12

OTHER ELIGIBILITY: Students interested in public service. Students holding an elected high school student body office or another qualifying elected position in their communities. U.S. citizen. Students intending to enroll in college within two years.

OVERVIEW: The U.S. Senate with sponsorship from the William Randolph Heart Foundation provides an annual educational program for students interested in learning about public service. High school principals and teachers nominate qualified students in the Fall. To qualify, students must hold an elected student body office or equivalent and show interest and aptitude in government, history and politics. Potential delegates are selected for their outstanding leadership skills, strong commitment to their schools and communities and academic achievements. Two students are selected from the pool of candidates from each state, Washington D.C. and the Defense Department Education Activity by the Chief State School Officer from that state or Department of Defense Education Activity. The 104 delegates will spend an all-expense paid week in Washington D.C. in March to watch the government at work and learn about public service. The delegates will hear policy addresses by Senators, cabinet members, officials from the Departments of State and Defense and directors of other federal agencies. In addition, they will participate in a meeting with a Justice of the U.S. Supreme Court. Each delegate will receive a college scholarship with encouragement to pursue courses in history and political science.

AWARD: $5,000 for each of the 104 delegates.

DEADLINE: Varies by state, but typically between August and November.

PROVIDER: U.S. Senate

WEBSITE: http://ussenateyouth.org

Washington Crossing Foundation National Scholarship

ELIGIBLE APPLICANT: Seniors

OTHER ELIGIBILITY: Students interested in a government service career. U.S. citizens.

OVERVIEW: An annual program to support students who are interested in a career in local, state or federal government service. Applicants include an essay (up to 300 words) on why they are planning a career in government service and how they were inspired from the leadership of George Washington in his crossing of the Delaware.

AWARD: $500 to $5,000. The number of awards varies.

DEADLINE: January

PROVIDER: The Washington Crossing Foundation

WEBSITE: www.gwcf.org

Women in Technology Scholarship

ELIGIBLE APPLICANT: Seniors

OTHER ELIGIBILITY: Female students interested in a career in computer science, information technology, computer engineering or related field. Students attending an accredited 2 year or 4 year college in the U.S.

OVERVIEW: An annual scholarship program for women intending to pursue a technology career in computer science, computer engineering, information technology or related field. Applicants are evaluated on academic achievement, involvement in community service, extracurricular activities, leadership, career path and their essay.

AWARD: up to $2,500. The number of awards varies.

DEADLINE: March

PROVIDER: Visionary Integration Professionals (VIP)

WEBSITE: www.trustvip.com/about-vip/community-support/women-technology-scholarship-wits

Chapter Seven

National Scholarships/ Random Drawing or Public Voting

This chapter contains national scholarships that are awarded based solely on a random drawing or public voting. For most of these scholarships, applicants are automatically entered into a random drawing when they register or open an account with the website. In some cases, applicants are required to answer questions or promote their entry or website campaign with the public to receive points, votes or additional entries for a random drawing. While these scholarships have a promotional component, they also provide awards to assist students with college tuition and other expenses.

The scholarships are listed in alphabetical order by scholarship name.

AFSA High School Scholarship Contest

ELIGIBLE APPLICANT: Seniors

OTHER ELIGIBILITY: U.S. citizen or legal resident who will attend an accredited two-year or four-year U.S. college or trade school.

OVERVIEW: Students read the "Fire Sprinkler" essay, register on the AFSA website and take a ten question multiple choice test about the essay. The test is open book. For each correct answer, the student receives one entry into a drawing. The maximum drawing entries is ten per student. The scholarship winners are selected by a random drawing.

AWARD: $2,000. Awards are provided to 10 winners.

DEADLINE: April 6, 2016

PROVIDER: American Fire Sprinkler Association

WEBSITE: www.afsascholarship.org/high-school-contest/hsstep1

Cappex $1,000 Easy College Money Scholarship

ELIGIBLE APPLICANT: Grades 9-12

OTHER ELIGIBILITY: U.S. citizen or permanent resident who will attend an accredited college in the U.S.

OVERVIEW: Students who create an account with this website are enter into random drawings for a scholarship.

AWARD: $1,000 for 1 winner every month.

DEADLINE: Monthly drawing

PROVIDER: Cappex

WEBSITE: www.cappex.com/scholarships/scholarshipDetails.jsp?scholarshipCode=gp

Chegg $1,000 Monthly Scholarship

ELIGIBLE APPLICANT: Age 16 and up

OTHER ELIGIBILITY: U.S. citizen or legal resident who will enroll in college in the U.S.

OVERVIEW: Students who create an account with this website and answer a quick question are entered into a random drawing for a scholarship.

AWARD: $1,000 for 1 winner every month.

DEADLINE: Monthly drawing

PROVIDER: Chegg

WEBSITE: www.chegg.com

CollegeWeekLive $5,000 Scholarship

ELIGIBLE APPLICANT: Grades 9-12

OTHER ELIGIBILITY: Students worldwide who will attend a CollegeWeekLive member college.

OVERVIEW: Students create an account with this website and visit at least five of the college pages. Students must login and participate in a CollegeWeekLive event during specific days. The winner is selected by a random drawing. Refer to the website for new scholarship opportunities.

AWARD: $5,000 for 1 winner.

DEADLINE: Refer to the website

PROVIDER: CollegeWeekLive

WEBSITE: www.collegeweeklive.com/scholarships

CollegeXPress $10,000 Scholarship Contest

ELIGIBLE APPLICANT: Seniors

OTHER ELIGIBILITY: U.S. citizen or legal resident who will attend one of the member colleges full-time in the Fall following high school graduation.

OVERVIEW: Students who create an account with this website are entered into a random drawing for a scholarship.

AWARD: $10,000 for the winner.

DEADLINE: Annual drawing in May

PROVIDER: CollegeXPress

WEBSITE: www.collegexpress.com/carnegie_scholarship

Discover Student Loans
$2,500 Scholarship Award

ELIGIBLE APPLICANT: Seniors

OTHER ELIGIBILITY: Citizen of the U.S. or Puerto Rico. Students who will attend an accredited non-profit four-year college in the U.S. or Puerto Rico.

OVERVIEW: Students who register with this website are entered into a random drawing for a scholarship. Students may earn up to three more entries by sharing this sweepstakes. One entry for a Facebook share, one entry for a Twitter share and one entry for an email share.

AWARD: $2,500 for 5 winners. There is a drawing every quarter.

DEADLINE: Quarterly drawing. Refer to the website for the next promotion period.

PROVIDER: Discover

WEBSITE: www.discover.com/student-loans/scholarships/ award.html

DoSomething.org Scholarships

ELIGIBLE APPLICANT: Grades 9-12

OTHER ELIGIBILITY: Citizen of the U.S. or Canada.

OVERVIEW: Students who participate in a campaign are entered into a random drawing for a scholarship. Refer to the website for current and future campaigns and requirements. New campaigns are added every quarter.

AWARD: Varies by campaign.

DEADLINE: Varies by campaign. Refer to the website.

PROVIDER: DoSomething.org

WEBSITE: www.dosomething.org/us/about/easy-scholarships

eCampusTours Scholarship Giveaway

ELIGIBLE APPLICANT: Seniors

OTHER ELIGIBILITY: U.S. citizen, national or permanent resident who will attend an accredited college in the U.S. within one year of receiving the award.

OVERVIEW: Students who create an account with this website are automatically entered into a scholarship program. The winners are selected by a random drawing.

AWARD: $1,000 for 2 winners.

DEADLINE: March 31, 2016

PROVIDER: eCampusTours

WEBSITE: www.ecampustours.com/scholarship-giveaway-registration.aspx

GoEnnounce $500 "Go Ennounce Yourself" Scholarship

ELIGIBLE APPLICANT: Grades 9-12

OTHER ELIGIBILITY: U.S. citizen or permanent legal resident who lives in Alabama, Arkansas, District of Columbia, Florida, Georgia, Maryland, Mississippi, North Carolina, South Carolina, Tennessee, Virginia or West Virginia who will enroll in an accredited two-year or four-year college in the U.S.

OVERVIEW: Students who create an account with this website are entered into a monthly random drawing for a scholarship. Students will be entered into the monthly drawing each month based on the scholastic and extracurricular progress and achievements that they post for that month.

AWARD: $500 for 1 winner every month.

DEADLINE: Drawing every month during the campaign.

PROVIDER: GoEnnounce

WEBSITE: www.goennounce.com/static/scholarship1

Harris Panel 2016 Annual Survey Research Sweepstakes

ELIGIBLE APPLICANT: Grades 9-12

OTHER ELIGIBILITY: Natural persons and legal residents of the U.S., Canada and the United Kingdom.

OVERVIEW: Students register and participate in online polls, questionnaires, surveys, focus groups and other market research activities. Students are entered into a random drawing every time they participate in a market research activity, subject to a maximum of thirty-five entries for each Bi-Weekly Period Drawing and two hundred entries for each Quarterly Period Drawing.

AWARD: $4,500 for the winner quarterly. $500 for the winner bi-weekly.

DEADLINE: Monthly and bi-weekly drawings.

PROVIDER: Harris Poll Online

WEBSITE: www1.pollg.com/Histakes/histakes.htm

NextStepU "Win Free College Tuition" Sweepstakes

ELIGIBLE APPLICANT: Grades 9-12

OTHER ELIGIBILITY: Legal residents of U.S. or Canada (excluding Puerto Rico and Quebec) who will enroll in college in three years from September 30, 2016.

OVERVIEW: Students who create an account with this website are entered into a random drawing for a scholarship.

AWARD: $2,500 for the winner.

DEADLINE: June 30, 2016

PROVIDER: NextStepU

WEBSITE: www.nextstepu.com/nextstepu-scholarships

Niche $500 High School Freshman Scholarship

ELIGIBLE APPLICANT: Freshmen

OTHER ELIGIBILITY: Class of 2019. U.S. citizen or legal resident. International students with valid visas are also eligible.

OVERVIEW: Students who create an account with this website are entered into a random drawing for a scholarship.

AWARD: $500 for the winner.

DEADLINE: June 1, 2016

PROVIDER: Niche

WEBSITE: https://colleges.niche.com/scholarship/high-school-freshman-scholarship/?source=f

Niche $500 High School Junior Scholarship

ELIGIBLE APPLICANT: Juniors

OTHER ELIGIBILITY: Class of 2017. U.S. citizen or legal resident. International students with valid visas are also eligible.

OVERVIEW: Students who create an account with this website are entered into a random drawing for a scholarship.

AWARD: $500 for the winner.

DEADLINE: June 1, 2016

PROVIDER: Niche

WEBSITE: https://colleges.niche.com/scholarship/high-school-junior-scholarship/?source=f

Niche $500 High School Senior Scholarship

ELIGIBLE APPLICANT: Seniors

OTHER ELIGIBILITY: Class of 2016. U.S. citizen or legal resident. International students with valid visas are also eligible.

OVERVIEW: Students who create an account with this website are entered into a random drawing for a scholarship.

AWARD: $500 for the winner.

DEADLINE: June 1, 2016

PROVIDER: Niche

WEBSITE: https://colleges.niche.com/scholarship/high-school-senior-scholarship/?source=f

Niche $500 High School Sophomore Scholarship

ELIGIBLE APPLICANT: Sophomores

OTHER ELIGIBILITY: Class of 2018. U.S. citizen or legal resident. International students with valid visas are also eligible.

OVERVIEW: Students who create an account with this website are entered into a random drawing for a scholarship.

AWARD: $500 for the winner.

DEADLINE: June 1, 2016

PROVIDER: Niche

WEBSITE: https://colleges.niche.com/scholarship/high-school-sophomore-scholarship/?source=f

Niche $2,000 “No Essay” College Scholarship

ELIGIBLE APPLICANT: Grades 9-12

OTHER ELIGIBILITY: U.S. citizen or legal resident who is enrolled in or within the next 12 months will enroll in a high school or college listed on nitche.com

OVERVIEW: Students who create an account with this website are entered into a monthly random drawing for a scholarship.

AWARD: $2,000 for 1 winner every month.

DEADLINE: Monthly drawing.

PROVIDER: Niche

WEBSITE: https://colleges.niche.com/scholarship/apply.aspx

SallieMae $1,000 Plan for College Sweepstakes

ELIGIBLE APPLICANT: Grades 9-12

OTHER ELIGIBILITY: U.S. citizen or legal resident.

OVERVIEW: Students who create an account with this website are entered into a monthly random drawing for a scholarship.

AWARD: $1,000 for 1 winner every month.

DEADLINE: Monthly drawing.

PROVIDER: SallieMae

WEBSITE: www.salliemae.com/student-loans/sweepstakes/college-answer-rules

ScholarshipPoints Scholarships

ELIGIBLE APPLICANT: Grades 9-12

OTHER ELIGIBILITY: U.S. citizen or legal resident.

OVERVIEW: Students who register and participate in contests, trivia, surveys and other activities earn points that can be used to enter into random drawings for scholarships. Refer to the website for current and future scholarship opportunities. There are points-based, activity-based and skills-based sweepstakes and contests.

AWARD: Varies by sweepstakes and contest.

DEADLINE: Varies by sweepstakes and contest. Refer to the website.

PROVIDER: ScholarshipPoints.com

WEBSITE: www.scholarshippoints.com/scholarship-contests

Student-View Scholarship

ELIGIBLE APPLICANT: Seniors

OTHER ELIGIBILITY: Students in the U.S.

OVERVIEW: Students who complete an online survey (15-25 minutes) about local colleges are entered into a random drawing for a scholarship.

AWARD: $4,000 for the winner. $1,000 for next 2 winners. $500 for 10 additional winners.

DEADLINE: April 22, 2016. Refer to the website for the next survey and deadline.

PROVIDER: Student Insights

WEBSITE: www.student-view.com/ScholarshipWmap.html

SunTrust Scholarship Sweepstakes

ELIGIBLE APPLICANT: Seniors

OTHER ELIGIBILITY: U.S. citizen or permanent legal resident who lives in Alabama, Arkansas, District of Columbia, Florida, Georgia, Maryland, Mississippi, North Carolina, South Carolina, Tennessee, Virginia or West Virginia who will enroll in an accredited two-year or four-year college in the U.S.

OVERVIEW: Students who complete an online entry form are entered into a random drawing for a scholarship.

AWARD: $500 for 2 winners every 2 weeks.

DEADLINE: Drawing every 2 weeks until May 13, 2016.

PROVIDER: SunTrust

WEBSITE: www.suntrusteducation.com/Scholarshipsweepstakes/index.html

SuperCollege $1,000 Scholarship

ELIGIBLE APPLICANT: Grades 9-12

OTHER ELIGIBILITY: U.S. citizen or legal resident.

OVERVIEW: Students who create an account with this website are entered into a random drawing for a scholarship.

AWARD: $1,000 for the winner.

DEADLINE: Refer to the website for the next application cycle.

PROVIDER: SuperCollege.com

WEBSITE: www.supercollege.com/scholarship

U.S. Bank Financial Genius Scholarship

ELIGIBLE APPLICANT: Seniors

OTHER ELIGIBILITY: Permanent legal resident of the U.S., excluding Florida, New York, Guam and Puerto Rico. Students who will enroll in an accredited two-year or four-year college in the Fall after high school graduation.

OVERVIEW: An annual promotion. For 2015, students who completed an application and viewed eight short modules were entered into a random drawing for a scholarship. The module topics were Savings and Investments, Mortgages, Overdraft, Payment Types and Credit Cards, Credit Scores and Reports, Insurance and Taxes, Financing Higher Education and Identity Protection. Refer to the website for the current promotion.

AWARD: $5,000 for 5 winners.

DEADLINE: Refer to the website for the next promotion period.

PROVIDER: U.S. Bank

WEBSITE: www.usbank.com/community/financial-education/scholarship.html

Chapter Eight

State Scholarships/
State Residency

Many college scholarships have state residency as an eligibility requirement. The search for these scholarships should begin with the Department of Education or a financial aid agency of your state government. The department or agency website has information on state financial aid programs and state scholarships that available from or promoted by the state. The website often includes additional resources for higher education, such as federal financial aid programs, college planning tips and information on student loans. Some of the websites even have a search engine for state scholarships.

Scholarships provided by the state often require students to enroll at a college within the state. Other types of state residency scholarships may or may not have this requirement.

In this chapter, we identified the Department of Education (or applicable agency) and its website address as the first item listed for each state. In addition, we included examples of private state residency scholarships for some states.

Alabama Commission on Higher Education

OVERVIEW: The state government. Refer to the Student Assistance page of the website for information on Alabama financial aid programs and grants. The website contains additional resources including information on Federal aid programs.

WEBSITE: www.ache.state.al.us

Horatio Alger State Scholarship

ELIGIBLE APPLICANT: Seniors

OTHER ELIGIBILITY: Alabama resident. 2.0 GPA. Financial Need ($55,000 or less adjusted gross family income). Overcome significant adversity. U.S. citizen who will attend an accredited not-for-profit college in the U.S. on a full-time basis.

OVERVIEW: This program provides financial aid to students who faced and overcame great obstacles. The application requires a detailed description and verification of the adversity. Students are also evaluated on their involvement in school and community service activities. Refer to the Scholarship Programs page of the website for additional information.

AWARD: $7,000 for 7 recipients.

DEADLINE: Refer to the website for the next application cycle.

PROVIDER: Horatio Alger Association of Distinguished Americans

WEBSITE: http://application.horatioalger.org

Alaska Commission on Postsecondary Education

OVERVIEW: The state government. Refer to the Financial Aid page of the website for information on Alaska financial aid programs and scholarships. This includes the Alaska Performance Scholarship for academic achievement in rigorous curriculum. The website contains additional resources including college planning tips.

WEBSITE: http://acpe.alaska.gov/FINANCIAL_AID

Horatio Alger State Scholarship

ELIGIBLE APPLICANT: Seniors

OTHER ELIGIBILITY: Alaska resident. Financial Need ($55,000 or less adjusted gross family income). 2.0 GPA. Overcome significant adversity. U.S. citizen who will attend an accredited not-for-profit college in the U.S. on a full-time basis.

OVERVIEW: This program provides financial aid to students who faced and overcame great obstacles. The application requires a detailed description and verification of the adversity. Students are also evaluated on their involvement in school and community service activities. Refer to the Scholarship Programs page of the website for additional information.

AWARD: $7,000 for 5 recipients.

DEADLINE: Refer to the website for the next application cycle.

PROVIDER: Horatio Alger Association of Distinguished Americans

WEBSITE: http://application.horatioalger.org

Arizona Department of Education

OVERVIEW: The state government. Refer to the Students page of the website for information on Arizona financial aid programs and scholarships.

WEBSITE: www.azed.gov/students

Horatio Alger State Scholarship

ELIGIBLE APPLICANT: Seniors

OTHER ELIGIBILITY: Arizona resident. Financial Need ($55,000 or less adjusted gross family income). 2.0 GPA. Overcome significant adversity. U.S. citizen who will attend an accredited not-for-profit college in the U.S. on a full-time basis.

OVERVIEW: This program provides financial aid to students who faced and overcame great obstacles. The application requires a detailed description and verification of the adversity. Students are also evaluated on their involvement in school and community service activities. Refer to the Scholarship Programs page of the website for additional information.

AWARD: $7,000 for 10 recipients.

DEADLINE: Refer to the website for the next application cycle.

PROVIDER: Horatio Alger Association of Distinguished Americans

WEBSITE: http://application.horatioalger.org

Arkansas Department of Higher Education

OVERVIEW: The state government. Refer to the Financial Aid page of the website for information on Arkansas financial aid programs and scholarships and other resources.

WEBSITE: http://scholarships.adhe.edu

Horatio Alger State Scholarship

ELIGIBLE APPLICANT: Seniors

OTHER ELIGIBILITY: Arkansas resident. Financial Need ($55,000 or less adjusted gross family income). 2.0 GPA. Overcome significant adversity. U.S. citizen who will attend an accredited not-for-profit college in the U.S. on a full-time basis.

OVERVIEW: This program provides financial aid to students who faced and overcame great obstacles. The application requires a detailed description and verification of the adversity. Students are also evaluated on their involvement in school and community service activities. Refer to the Scholarship Programs page of the website for additional information.

AWARD: $7,000 for 7 recipients.

DEADLINE: Refer to the website for the next application cycle.

PROVIDER: Horatio Alger Association of Distinguished Americans

WEBSITE: http://application.horatioalger.org

California Student Aid Commission

OVERVIEW: The state government. Refer to the Students & Parents page of the website for information on California financial aid programs, scholarships and other resources.

WEBSITE: www.csac.ca.gov

Bright Minds Scholarships

ELIGIBLE APPLICANT: Seniors

OTHER ELIGIBILITY: California residents who lives within a Pacific Gas & Electric service area. Students who will attend an accredited two-year or four-year college in the Fall after high school graduation.

OVERVIEW: An annual scholarship program with a preference for students who intend to major in a STEM (Science, Technology, Engineering, Math) field. Applicants will be evaluated on academic achievement, financial need, leadership and community service. Refer to the website for a list of service areas.

AWARD: Ten recipients will receive up to $20,000 renewable annually for up to five years. Ninety recipients will receive a one-time award of $2,000.

DEADLINE: February annually. Refer to the website for the next application cycle.

PROVIDER: Pacific Gas and Electric Company

WEBSITE: www.pge.com/en/about/community/signatureprograms/education/brightminds/index.page

Edison International Scholars

ELIGIBLE APPLICANT: Senior

OTHER ELIGIBILITY: California residents in a Southern California Edison service territory. 3.0 GPA. Financial Need. Students planning to major in a STEM field and enroll full-time in an accredit 4 year U.S. college.

OVERVIEW: To award scholarships to students who plan to major in a STEM (Science, Technology, Engineering, Math) field. Preference will be given to students who are first-generation college students or have overcome significant obstacles and challenges. Refer to the website for eligible areas.

AWARD: $10,000 renewable over 4 years. Up to 30 awards are provided.

DEADLINE: February annually

PROVIDER: Edison International

WEBSITE: www.edison.com/home/community/edison-scholars.html

Horatio Alger State Scholarship

ELIGIBLE APPLICANT: Seniors

OTHER ELIGIBILITY: California resident. Financial Need ($55,000 or less adjusted gross family income). 2.0 GPA. Overcome significant adversity. U.S. citizen who will attend a U.S. accredited not-for-profit college full-time.

OVERVIEW: This program provides financial aid to students who faced and overcame great obstacles. The application requires a detailed description and verification of the adversity. Students are also evaluated on their involvement in school and community service activities. Refer to the Scholarship Programs page of the website for additional information.

AWARD: $7,000 for 92 recipients.

DEADLINE: Refer to the website for the next application cycle.

PROVIDER: Horatio Alger Association of Distinguished Americans

WEBSITE: http://application.horatioalger.org

Colorado Department of Higher Education

OVERVIEW: The state government. Refer to the Students & Parents page of the website for information on Colorado financial aid programs, scholarships and other resources.

WEBSITE: http://highered.colorado.gov/finance/financialaid/#

Horatio Alger State Scholarship

ELIGIBLE APPLICANT: Seniors

OTHER ELIGIBILITY: Colorado resident. Financial Need ($55,000 or less adjusted gross family income). 2.0 GPA. Overcome significant adversity. U.S. citizen who will attend an accredited not-for-profit college in the U.S. on a full-time basis.

OVERVIEW: This program provides financial aid to students who faced and overcame great obstacles. The application requires a detailed description and verification of the adversity. Students are also evaluated on their involvement in school and community service activities. Refer to the Scholarship Programs page of the website for additional information.

AWARD: $7,000 for 9 recipients.

DEADLINE: Refer to the website for the next application cycle.

PROVIDER: Horatio Alger Association of Distinguished Americans

WEBSITE: http://application.horatioalger.org

Connecticut Office of Higher Education

OVERVIEW: The state government. Refer to the Students & Families page of the website for information on Connecticut financial aid programs, scholarships and other resources. The state offers a Governor's Need-Based Scholarship and a Governor's Need & Merit-Based Scholarship.

WEBSITE: www.ctohe.org/SFA/default.shtml

Horatio Alger State Scholarship

ELIGIBLE APPLICANT: Seniors

OTHER ELIGIBILITY: Connecticut resident. Financial Need ($55,000 or less adjusted gross family income). 2.0 GPA. Overcome significant adversity. U.S. citizen who will attend an accredited not-for-profit college in the U.S. on a full-time basis.

OVERVIEW: This program provides financial aid to students who faced and overcame great obstacles. The application requires a detailed description and verification of the adversity. Students are also evaluated on their involvement in school and community service activities. Refer to the Scholarship Programs page of the website for additional information.

AWARD: $7,000 for 6 recipients.

DEADLINE: Refer to the website for the next application cycle.

PROVIDER: Horatio Alger Association of Distinguished Americans

WEBSITE: http://application.horatioalger.org

Shaw-Worth Memorial Scholarship

ELIGIBLE APPLICANT: Seniors

OTHER ELIGIBILITY: Connecticut resident.

OVERVIEW: This program rewards New England students who work with and on behalf of animals. Examples include leadership in animal protection organizations and rescue of animals in danger. Applicants write a letter which includes a description of their achievements in animal protection, attitude toward animals, a description of their activities to promote animal protection and their plans for future animal protection work.

AWARD: up to $3,500. The number of awards varies.

DEADLINE: March. Refer to the website for the next application cycle.

PROVIDER: The Humane Society of the United States

WEBSITE: www.humanesociety.org/parents_educators/teens/shaw_worth_scholarship.html

Stephen Phillips Memorial Scholarship Fund

ELIGIBLE APPLICANT: Seniors

OTHER ELIGIBILITY: Connecticut resident. 3.0 GPA. Financial Need. U.S. citizen or permanent resident. Students who will attend an accredited four-year college in the U.S.

OVERVIEW: An annual memorial scholarship for New England students with financial need who display high academic, citizenship and character achievements. Refer to the website for a financial need eligibility calculator.

AWARD: $3,000 to $18,000 renewable annually. The number of awards varies, but approximately 140 awards were provided in 2015.

DEADLINE: April for early applications. May for general applications.

PROVIDER: The Stephen Phillips Memorial Scholarship Fund, Inc.

WEBSITE: www.phillips-scholarship.org/about-us/history-of-the-award

Delaware Department of Education

OVERVIEW: The state government. Refer to the Higher Education page of the website for information on Delaware financial aid programs and scholarships.

WEBSITE: www.doe.k12.de.us/Page/316

Horatio Alger State Scholarship

ELIGIBLE APPLICANT: Seniors

OTHER ELIGIBILITY: Delaware resident. Financial Need ($55,000 or less adjusted gross family income). 2.0 GPA. Overcome significant adversity. U.S. citizen who will attend an accredited not-for-profit college in the U.S. on a full-time basis.

OVERVIEW: This program provides financial aid to students who faced and overcame great obstacles. The application requires a detailed description and verification of the adversity. Students are also evaluated on their involvement in school and community service activities. Refer to the Scholarship Programs page of the website for additional information.

AWARD: $7,000 for 14 recipients.

DEADLINE: Refer to the website for the next application cycle.

PROVIDER: Horatio Alger Association of Distinguished Americans

WEBSITE: http://application.horatioalger.org

Office of the State Superintendent of Education

OVERVIEW: The state government. Refer to the Programs; Postsecondary Education page of the website for information on District of Columbia financial aid programs, scholarships and other resources, such as federal aid programs.

WEBSITE: www.seo.dc.gov

Horatio Alger State Scholarship

ELIGIBLE APPLICANT: Seniors

OTHER ELIGIBILITY: District of Columbia resident. Financial Need ($55,000 or less adjusted gross family income). 2.0 GPA. Overcome significant adversity. U.S. citizen who will attend an accredited not-for-profit college in the U.S. on a full-time basis.

OVERVIEW: This program provides financial aid to students who faced and overcame great obstacles. The application requires a detailed description and verification of the adversity. Students are also evaluated on their involvement in school and community service activities. Refer to the Scholarship Programs page of the website for additional information.

AWARD: $7,000. The number of awards varies.

DEADLINE: Refer to the website for the next application cycle.

PROVIDER: Horatio Alger Association of Distinguished Americans

WEBSITE: http://application.horatioalger.org

Florida Department of Education

OVERVIEW: The state government. Refer to the Higher Education page of the website then Office of Student Financial Assistance for information on Florida financial aid programs, scholarships, student loans and other resources. This includes the Florida Bright Futures Scholarship.

WEBSITE: www.floridastudentfinancialaid.org

Barnes Scholarship

ELIGIBLE APPLICANT: Seniors

OTHER ELIGIBILITY: Florida resident of Citrus, Hernando, Pasco, Pinellas and Hillsborough Counties. Financial Need. 3.0 GPA. Overcome significant obstacles in life. U.S. citizen or permanent resident.

OVERVIEW: An annual scholarship program for Tampa Bay area students who are high academic achievers, have overcome significant obstacles in their lives and have financial need. Preference will be given to students whose parents have not graduated from college and who want to attend college outside of Florida.

AWARD: up to $15,000 renewable annually (up to 60,000 total) for 4 recipients.

DEADLINE: October. Refer to the website for the next application cycle.

PROVIDER: Tampa Bay Times Fund, Inc.

WEBSITE: www.tampabay.com/company/times-fund/barnes-about

Horatio Alger State Scholarship

ELIGIBLE APPLICANT: Seniors

OTHER ELIGIBILITY: Florida resident. Financial Need ($55,000 or less adjusted gross family income). 2.0 GPA. Overcome significant adversity. U.S. citizen who will attend an accredited not-for-profit college in the U.S.

OVERVIEW: This program provides financial aid to students who faced and overcame great obstacles. The application requires a detailed description and verification of the adversity. Students are also evaluated on their involvement in school and community service activities. Refer to the Scholarship Programs page of the website for additional information.

AWARD: $7,000 for 43 recipients.

DEADLINE: Refer to the website for the next application cycle.

PROVIDER: Horatio Alger Association of Distinguished Americans

WEBSITE: http://application.horatioalger.org

Salute To Education Scholarship

ELIGIBLE APPLICANT: Seniors

OTHER ELIGIBILITY: Florida resident of Miami-Dade or Broward County. Financial Need. 3.0 GPA. U.S. citizen or permanent resident.

OVERVIEW: An annual scholarship program for Southern Florida students. Applicants can enter only one category. The categories are Leadership Service, Natural Sciences, Math & Computer Sciences, Athletics, Performance Arts & Visual Arts, and Foreign Language & Language Arts. Students are evaluated on academics, financial need, involvement in school and community activities, leadership and other criteria.

AWARD: $1,500 for 100 recipients.

DEADLINE: February. Refer to the website for the next application cycle.

PROVIDER: Ford and Lincoln Dealers and Ford Motor Company

WEBSITE: www.stescholarships.org/AU_home-en.html

Georgia Student Finance Commission

OVERVIEW: The state government. Refer to the Programs & Regulations page of the website for information on Georgia financial aid programs, scholarships and student loans.

WEBSITE: www.gsfc.org

Horatio Alger State Scholarship

ELIGIBLE APPLICANT: Seniors

OTHER ELIGIBILITY: Georgia resident. Financial Need ($55,000 or less adjusted gross family income). 2.0 GPA. Overcome significant adversity. U.S. citizen who will attend an accredited not-for-profit college in the U.S. on a full-time basis.

OVERVIEW: This program provides financial aid to students who faced and overcame great obstacles. The application requires a detailed description and verification of the adversity. Students are also evaluated on their involvement in school and community service activities. Refer to the Scholarship Programs page of the website for additional information.

AWARD: $7,000 for 50 recipients.

DEADLINE: Refer to the website for the next application cycle.

PROVIDER: Horatio Alger Association of Distinguished Americans

WEBSITE: http://application.horatioalger.org

Hawaii State Department of Education

OVERVIEW: The state government. Refer to the Teaching & Learning page then College & Career Readiness page of the website for information on Hawaii financial aid programs, scholarships, college preparation tips and other resources.

WEBSITE: www.hawaiipublicschools.org

Horatio Alger State Scholarship

ELIGIBLE APPLICANT: Seniors

OTHER ELIGIBILITY: Hawaii resident. Financial Need ($55,000 or less adjusted gross family income). 2.0 GPA. Overcome significant adversity. U.S. citizen who will attend an accredited not-for-profit college in the U.S. on a full-time basis.

OVERVIEW: This program provides financial aid to students who faced and overcame great obstacles. The application requires a detailed description and verification of the adversity. Students are also evaluated on their involvement in school and community service activities. Refer to the Scholarship Programs page of the website for additional information.

AWARD: $7,000 for 5 recipients.

DEADLINE: Refer to the website for the next application cycle.

PROVIDER: Horatio Alger Association of Distinguished Americans

WEBSITE: http://application.horatioalger.org

Idaho State Board of Education

OVERVIEW: The state government. Refer to the Scholarships page of the website for information on Idaho financial aid programs and scholarships.

WEBSITE: https://boardofed.idaho.gov/scholarship/scholarship_jump.asp

Horatio Alger State Scholarship

ELIGIBLE APPLICANT: Seniors

OTHER ELIGIBILITY: Idaho resident. Financial Need ($55,000 or less adjusted gross family income). 2.0 GPA. Overcome significant adversity. U.S. citizen who will attend an accredited not-for-profit college in Idaho on a full-time basis.

OVERVIEW: This program provides financial aid to students who faced and overcame great obstacles. The application requires a detailed description and verification of the adversity. Students are also evaluated on their involvement in school and community service activities. Refer to the Scholarship Programs page of the website for additional information.

AWARD: $7,000 for 25 recipients.

DEADLINE: Refer to the website for the next application cycle.

PROVIDER: Horatio Alger Association of Distinguished Americans

WEBSITE: http://application.horatioalger.org

Illinois Student Assistance Commission

OVERVIEW: The state government. Refer to the Students & Parents page of the website for information on Illinois financial aid programs, scholarships, college planning tips and other resources.

WEBSITE: www.isac.org

Back 2 School Illinois Scholarship

ELIGIBLE APPLICANT: Seniors

OTHER ELIGIBILITY: Illinois resident. U.S. citizens or permanent resident. Students enrolling in a two-year or four-year college in the U.S.

OVERVIEW: An annual scholarship program for Illinois students who excel academically and show leadership in school and local community involvement.

AWARD: $2,500 for 5 recipients.

DEADLINE: April

PROVIDER: Community Currency Exchange Association of Illinois and the Tufano Family.

WEBSITE: www.b2si.org/programs/college-scholarship

Champion Scholars Scholarship

ELIGIBLE APPLICANT: Seniors

OTHER ELIGIBILITY: Illinois resident. 3.0 GPA. Students who will attend an accredited two-year or four-year college.

OVERVIEW: An annual scholarship program for students in five states. Students are evaluated on academic achievement, awards, volunteerism and their response to the essay question "What makes you a champion in your school or in your community?"

AWARD: $5,000 to the winner. $3,000 for 2nd place. $2,000 for 3rd place.

DEADLINE: April

PROVIDER: Champion Energy Services

WEBSITE: www.championenergyservices.com/programs/scholarship

Horatio Alger State Scholarship

ELIGIBLE APPLICANT: Seniors

OTHER ELIGIBILITY: Illinois resident. Financial Need ($55,000 or less adjusted gross family income). 2.0 GPA. Overcome significant adversity. U.S. citizen who will attend an accredited not-for-profit college in the U.S. on a full-time basis.

OVERVIEW: This program provides financial aid to students who faced and overcame great obstacles. The application requires a detailed description and verification of the adversity. Students are also evaluated on their involvement in school and community service activities. Refer to the Scholarship Programs page of the website for additional information.

AWARD: $7,000 for 20 recipients.

DEADLINE: Refer to the website for the next application cycle.

PROVIDER: Horatio Alger Association of Distinguished Americans

WEBSITE: http://application.horatioalger.org

Indiana Commission for Higher Education

OVERVIEW: The state government. Refer to the Scholar Track page of the website for information on Indiana financial aid programs and scholarships.

WEBSITE: www.in.gov/ssaci

Horatio Alger State Scholarship

ELIGIBLE APPLICANT: Seniors

OTHER ELIGIBILITY: Indiana resident. Financial Need ($55,000 or less adjusted gross family income). 2.0 GPA. Overcome significant adversity. U.S. citizen who will attend an accredited not-for-profit college in the U.S. on a full-time basis.

OVERVIEW: This program provides financial aid to students who faced and overcame great obstacles. The application requires a detailed description and verification of the adversity. Students are also evaluated on their involvement in school and community service activities. Refer to the Scholarship Programs page of the website for additional information.

AWARD: $7,000 for 10 recipients.

DEADLINE: Refer to the website for the next application cycle.

PROVIDER: Horatio Alger Association of Distinguished Americans

WEBSITE: http://application.horatioalger.org

Iowa College Student Aid Commission

OVERVIEW: The state government. Refer to the website for information on Iowa financial aid programs, scholarships, college planning tips, student loans and other resources.

WEBSITE: www.iowacollegeaid.gov

Horatio Alger State Scholarship

ELIGIBLE APPLICANT: Seniors

OTHER ELIGIBILITY: Idaho resident. Financial Need ($55,000 or less adjusted gross family income). 2.0 GPA. Overcome significant adversity. U.S. citizen who will attend an accredited not-for-profit college in the U.S. on a full-time basis.

OVERVIEW: This program provides financial aid to students who faced and overcame great obstacles. The application requires a detailed description and verification of the adversity. Students are also evaluated on their involvement in school and community service activities. Refer to the Scholarship Programs page of the website for additional information.

AWARD: $6,000 to $7,000. The number of awards varies.

DEADLINE: Refer to the website for the next application cycle.

PROVIDER: Horatio Alger Association of Distinguished Americans

WEBSITE: http://application.horatioalger.org

Kansas Board of Regents

OVERVIEW: The state government. Refer to the Students page of the website for information on Kansas financial aid programs, scholarships and other resources.

WEBSITE: www.kansasregents.org

Horatio Alger State Scholarship

ELIGIBLE APPLICANT: Seniors

OTHER ELIGIBILITY: Kansas resident. Financial Need ($55,000 or less adjusted gross family income). 2.0 GPA. Overcome significant adversity. U.S. citizen who will attend an accredited not-for-profit college in the U.S. on a full-time basis.

OVERVIEW: This program provides financial aid to students who faced and overcame great obstacles. The application requires a detailed description and verification of the adversity. Students are also evaluated on their involvement in school and community service activities. Refer to the Scholarship Programs page of the website for additional information.

AWARD: $7,000 for 5 recipients.

DEADLINE: Refer to the website for the next application cycle.

PROVIDER: Horatio Alger Association of Distinguished Americans

WEBSITE: http://application.horatioalger.org

Kentucky Higher Education Assistance Authority

OVERVIEW: The state government. Refer to the website for information on Kentucky financial aid programs, scholarships, federal aid programs and other resources.

WEBSITE: www.kheaa.com

Horatio Alger State Scholarship

ELIGIBLE APPLICANT: Seniors

OTHER ELIGIBILITY: Kentucky resident. Financial Need ($55,000 or less adjusted gross family income). 2.0 GPA. Overcome significant adversity. U.S. citizen who will attend an accredited not-for-profit college in the U.S. on a full-time basis.

OVERVIEW: This program provides financial aid to students who faced and overcame great obstacles. The application requires a detailed description and verification of the adversity. Students are also evaluated on their involvement in school and community service activities. Refer to the Scholarship Programs page of the website for additional information.

AWARD: $7,000 for 8 recipients.

DEADLINE: Refer to the website for the next application cycle.

PROVIDER: Horatio Alger Association of Distinguished Americans

WEBSITE: http://application.horatioalger.org

Louisiana Office of Student Financial Assistance

OVERVIEW: The state government. Refer to the website for information on Louisiana financial aid programs, scholarships, college planning tips and other resources.

WEBSITE: www.osfa.la.gov

Horatio Alger State Scholarship

ELIGIBLE APPLICANT: Seniors

OTHER ELIGIBILITY: Louisiana resident. Financial Need ($55,000 or less adjusted gross family income). 2.0 GPA. Overcome significant adversity. U.S. citizen who will attend an accredited not-for-profit college in Louisiana on a full-time basis.

OVERVIEW: This program provides financial aid to students who faced and overcame great obstacles. The application requires a detailed description and verification of the adversity. Students are also evaluated on their involvement in school and community service activities. Refer to the Scholarship Programs page of the website for additional information.

AWARD: $10,500 for 25 recipients.

DEADLINE: Refer to the website for the next application cycle.

PROVIDER: Horatio Alger Association of Distinguished Americans

WEBSITE: http://application.horatioalger.org

Finance Authority of Maine

OVERVIEW: The state government. Refer to the Education page of the website for information on Maine financial aid programs, scholarships, student loans and other resources.

WEBSITE: www.famemaine.com/education/topics/paying-for-college

Horatio Alger State Scholarship

ELIGIBLE APPLICANT: Seniors

OTHER ELIGIBILITY: Maine resident. Financial Need ($55,000 or less adjusted gross family income). 2.0 GPA. Overcome significant adversity. U.S. citizen who will attend an accredited not-for-profit college in the U.S. on a full-time basis.

OVERVIEW: This program provides financial aid to students who faced and overcame great obstacles. The application requires a detailed description and verification of the adversity. Students are also evaluated on their involvement in school and community service activities. Refer to the Scholarship Programs page of the website for additional information.

AWARD: $7,000 for 5 recipients.

DEADLINE: Refer to the website for the next application cycle.

PROVIDER: Horatio Alger Association of Distinguished Americans

WEBSITE: http://application.horatioalger.org

Shaw-Worth Memorial Scholarship

ELIGIBLE APPLICANT: Seniors

OTHER ELIGIBILITY: Connecticut resident.

OVERVIEW: This program rewards New England students who work with and on behalf of animals. Examples include leadership in animal protection organizations and rescue of animals in danger. Applicants write a letter which includes a description of their achievements in animal protection, attitude toward animals, a description of their activities to promote animal protection and their plans for future animal protection work.

AWARD: up to $3,500. The number of awards varies.

DEADLINE: March. Refer to the website for the next application cycle.

PROVIDER: The Humane Society of the United States

WEBSITE: www.humanesociety.org/parents_educators/teens/shaw_worth_scholarship.html

Stephen Phillips Memorial Scholarship Fund

ELIGIBLE APPLICANT: Seniors

OTHER ELIGIBILITY: Maine resident. 3.0 GPA. Financial Need. U.S. citizen or permanent resident. Students who will attend an accredited four-year college in the U.S.

OVERVIEW: An annual memorial scholarship for New England students with financial need who display high academic, citizenship and character achievements. Refer to the website for a financial need eligibility calculator.

AWARD: $3,000 to $18,000 renewable annually. The number of awards varies, but approximately 140 awards were provided in 2015.

DEADLINE: April for early applications. May for general applications.

PROVIDER: The Stephen Phillips Memorial Scholarship Fund, Inc.

WEBSITE: www.phillips-scholarship.org/about-us/history-of-the-award

Maryland Higher Education Commission

OVERVIEW: The state government. The state legislative branch offers Delegate Scholarships and a Senatorial Scholarships. The Howard P. Rawlings of Educational Excellence Awards provides a need-based scholarship and a combined need & merit-based scholarship. There are additional scholarships for unique situations. Refer to the state website for Maryland financial aid programs, scholarships, college preparation tips and other resources.

WEBSITE: www.mhec.state.md.us/FinancialAid/descriptions.asp

Horatio Alger State Scholarship

ELIGIBLE APPLICANT: Seniors

OTHER ELIGIBILITY: Maryland resident. Financial Need ($55,000 or less adjusted gross family income). 2.0 GPA. Overcome significant adversity. U.S. citizen who will attend an accredited not-for-profit college in the U.S. on a full-time basis.

OVERVIEW: This program provides financial aid to students who faced and overcame great obstacles. The application requires a detailed description and verification of the adversity. Students are also evaluated on their involvement in school and community service activities. Refer to the Scholarship Programs page of the website for additional information.

AWARD: $7,000. The number of awards varies.

DEADLINE: Refer to the website for the next application cycle.

PROVIDER: Horatio Alger Association of Distinguished Americans

WEBSITE: http://application.horatioalger.org

Massachusetts Department of Higher Education Office of Student Financial Assistance

OVERVIEW: The state government. Refer to the website for information on Massachusetts financial aid programs, scholarships, college planning tips, federal aid programs and other resources.

WEBSITE: www.osfa.mass.edu

Horatio Alger State Scholarship

ELIGIBLE APPLICANT: Seniors

OTHER ELIGIBILITY: Massachusetts resident. Financial Need ($55,000 or less adjusted gross family income). 2.0 GPA. Overcome significant adversity. U.S. citizen who will attend an accredited not-for-profit college in the U.S. on a full-time basis.

OVERVIEW: This program provides financial aid to students who faced and overcame great obstacles. The application requires a detailed description and verification of the adversity. Students are also evaluated on their involvement in school and community service activities. Refer to the Scholarship Programs page of the website for additional information.

AWARD: $7,000 for 10 recipients.

DEADLINE: Refer to the website for the next application cycle.

PROVIDER: Horatio Alger Association of Distinguished Americans

WEBSITE: http://application.horatioalger.org

Shaw-Worth Memorial Scholarship

ELIGIBLE APPLICANT: Seniors

OTHER ELIGIBILITY: Connecticut resident.

OVERVIEW: This program rewards New England students who work with and on behalf of animals. Examples include leadership in animal protection organizations and rescue of animals in danger. Applicants write a letter which includes a description of their achievements in animal protection, attitude toward animals, a description of their activities to promote animal protection and their plans for future animal protection work.

AWARD: up to $3,500. The number of awards varies.

DEADLINE: March. Refer to the website for the next application cycle.

PROVIDER: The Humane Society of the United States

WEBSITE: www.humanesociety.org/parents_educators/teens/shaw_worth_scholarship.html

Stephen Phillips Memorial Scholarship Fund

ELIGIBLE APPLICANT: Seniors

OTHER ELIGIBILITY: Massachusetts resident. 3.0 GPA. Financial Need. U.S. citizen or permanent resident. Students who will attend an accredited four-year college in the U.S.

OVERVIEW: An annual memorial scholarship for New England students with financial need who display high academic, citizenship and character achievements. Refer to the website for a financial need eligibility calculator.

AWARD: $3,000 to $18,000 renewable annually. The number of awards varies, but approximately 140 awards were provided in 2015.

DEADLINE: April for early applications. May for general applications.

PROVIDER: The Stephen Phillips Memorial Scholarship Fund, Inc.

WEBSITE: www.phillips-scholarship.org/about-us/history-of-the-award

Michigan Student Financial Service Bureau

OVERVIEW: The state government. Refer to the website for information on Michigan financial aid programs, scholarships, student loans and other resources.

WEBSITE: www.michigan.gov/mistudentaid

Horatio Alger State Scholarship

ELIGIBLE APPLICANT: Seniors

OTHER ELIGIBILITY: Michigan resident. Financial Need ($55,000 or less adjusted gross family income). 2.0 GPA. Overcome significant adversity. U.S. citizen who will attend an accredited not-for-profit college in the U.S. on a full-time basis.

OVERVIEW: This program provides financial aid to students who faced and overcame great obstacles. The application requires a detailed description and verification of the adversity. Students are also evaluated on their involvement in school and community service activities. Refer to the Scholarship Programs page of the website for additional information.

AWARD: $7,000 for 15 recipients.

DEADLINE: Refer to the website for the next application cycle.

PROVIDER: Horatio Alger Association of Distinguished Americans

WEBSITE: http://application.horatioalger.org

Minnesota Office of Higher Education

OVERVIEW: The state government. Refer to the website for information on Minnesota financial aid programs, scholarships, college planning tips and other resources.

WEBSITE: www.ohe.state.mn.us

Catch A Break Scholarship

ELIGIBLE APPLICANT: Seniors

OTHER ELIGIBILITY: Minnesota resident. Financial Need. 2.5 GPA. 24 on ACT. U.S. citizen who will attend an accredited four-year college in Minnesota. Plan to live on campus.

OVERVIEW: A scholarship program for students enrolling at a Minnesota college. Recipients are selected basis on academic achievements, financial need, demonstrated leadership, participation in school and community activities, honors, work experience, statement of goals, unusual personal or family circumstances and an essay.

AWARD: Up to $10,000 renewable annually (up to $40,000 total). The number of awards varies.

DEADLINE: February 16, 2016. Refer to the website for the next deadline.

PROVIDER: Scholarship America

WEBSITE: http://sms.scholarshipamerica.org/catchabreak/index.html

Horatio Alger State Scholarship

ELIGIBLE APPLICANT: Seniors

OTHER ELIGIBILITY: Minnesota resident. Financial Need ($55,000 or less adjusted gross family income). 2.0 GPA. Overcome significant adversity. U.S. citizen who will attend an accredited not-for-profit college in the U.S. on a full-time basis.

OVERVIEW: This program provides financial aid to students who faced and overcame great obstacles. The application requires a detailed description and verification of the adversity. Students are also evaluated on their involvement in school and community service activities. Refer to the Scholarship Programs page of the website for additional information.

AWARD: $7,000 to $20,000. The number of awards varies.

DEADLINE: Refer to the website for the next application cycle.

PROVIDER: Horatio Alger Association of Distinguished Americans

WEBSITE: http://application.horatioalger.org

Mississippi Office of Student Financial Aid

OVERVIEW: The state government. Refer to the website for information on Mississippi financial aid programs, scholarships, college planning tips and other resources.

WEBSITE: www.mississippi.edu/riseupms

Horatio Alger State Scholarship

ELIGIBLE APPLICANT: Seniors

OTHER ELIGIBILITY: Mississippi resident. Financial Need ($55,000 or less adjusted gross family income). 2.0 GPA. Overcome significant adversity. U.S. citizen who will attend an accredited not-for-profit college in the U.S. on a full-time basis.

OVERVIEW: This program provides financial aid to students who faced and overcame great obstacles. The application requires a detailed description and verification of the adversity. Students are also evaluated on their involvement in school and community service activities. Refer to the Scholarship Programs page of the website for additional information.

AWARD: $7,000 for 5 recipients.

DEADLINE: Refer to the website for the next application cycle.

PROVIDER: Horatio Alger Association of Distinguished Americans

WEBSITE: http://application.horatioalger.org

Missouri Department of Higher Education

OVERVIEW: The state government. Refer to the website for information on Missouri financial aid programs, scholarships, college planning tips and other resources.

WEBSITE: www.dhe.mo.gov

James & Nellie Westlake Scholarship Foundation

ELIGIBLE APPLICANT: Seniors

OTHER ELIGIBILITY: Missouri resident. Financial Need (defined as adjusted gross family income of $50,000 or less and expected family contribution toward college of $7,000 or less). U.S. citizen who will enroll full-time at an accredited four-year college.

OVERVIEW: Recipients are selected basis on academic achievements, financial need, demonstrated leadership, participation in school and community activities, honors, work experience, statement of goals, unusual personal or family circumstances and other criteria.

AWARD: The cost of tuition. In addition, approximately $2,000 to cover the cost of fees, books, and supplies. The award is renewable annually. The number of awards is unknown.

DEADLINE: Typically February.

PROVIDER: James L. and Nellie M. Westlake Scholarship Foundation

WEBSITE: www.scholarsapply.org/westlake

Horatio Alger State Scholarship

ELIGIBLE APPLICANT: Seniors

OTHER ELIGIBILITY: Missouri resident. Financial Need ($55,000 or less adjusted gross family income). 2.0 GPA. Overcome significant adversity. U.S. citizen who will attend an accredited not-for-profit college in the U.S. on a full-time basis.

OVERVIEW: This program provides financial aid to students who faced and overcame great obstacles. The application requires a detailed description and verification of the adversity. Students are also evaluated on their involvement in school and community service activities. Refer to the Scholarship Programs page of the website for additional information.

AWARD: $7,000 for 5 recipients.

DEADLINE: Refer to the website for the next application cycle.

PROVIDER: Horatio Alger Association of Distinguished Americans

WEBSITE: http://application.horatioalger.org

Montana University System

OVERVIEW: The state government. Refer to the Scholarship page of the website for information on Montana financial aid programs, scholarships, college planning tips and other resources.

WEBSITE: http://mus.edu/Prepare/Pay/Scholarships/default.asp

Horatio Alger State Scholarship

ELIGIBLE APPLICANT: Seniors

OTHER ELIGIBILITY: Montana resident. Financial Need ($55,000 or less adjusted gross family income). 2.0 GPA. Overcome significant adversity. U.S. citizen who will attend an accredited not-for-profit college in Montana on a full-time basis.

OVERVIEW: This program provides financial aid to students who faced and overcame great obstacles. The application requires a detailed description and verification of the adversity. Students are also evaluated on their involvement in school and community service activities. Refer to the Scholarship Programs page of the website for additional information.

AWARD: $7,000 for 50 recipients.

DEADLINE: Refer to the website for the next application cycle.

PROVIDER: Horatio Alger Association of Distinguished Americans

WEBSITE: http://application.horatioalger.org

Nebraska Coordinating Commission for Postsecondary Education

OVERVIEW: The state government. Refer to the Financial Aid page of the website for information on Nebraska financial aid programs and scholarships.

WEBSITE: https://ccpe.nebraska.gov

Horatio Alger State Scholarship

ELIGIBLE APPLICANT: Seniors

OTHER ELIGIBILITY: Nebraska resident. Financial Need ($55,000 or less adjusted gross family income). 2.0 GPA. Overcome significant adversity. U.S. citizen who will attend an accredited not-for-profit college in the U.S. on a full-time basis.

OVERVIEW: This program provides financial aid to students who faced and overcame great obstacles. The application requires a detailed description and verification of the adversity. Students are also evaluated on their involvement in school and community service activities. Refer to the Scholarship Programs page of the website for additional information.

AWARD: $6,000. The number of awards varies.

DEADLINE: Refer to the website for the next application cycle.

PROVIDER: Horatio Alger Association of Distinguished Americans

WEBSITE: http://application.horatioalger.org

Nevada Department of Education

OVERVIEW: The state government. Refer to the Nevada Scholarship Choice Page of the website for information on Nevada scholarships.

WEBSITE: www.doe.nv.gov

Horatio Alger State Scholarship

ELIGIBLE APPLICANT: Seniors

OTHER ELIGIBILITY: Nevada resident. Financial Need ($55,000 or less adjusted gross family income). 2.0 GPA. Overcome significant adversity. U.S. citizen who will attend an accredited not-for-profit college in the U.S. on a full-time basis.

OVERVIEW: This program provides financial aid to students who faced and overcame great obstacles. The application requires a detailed description and verification of the adversity. Students are also evaluated on their involvement in school and community service activities. Refer to the Scholarship Programs page of the website for additional information.

AWARD: $7,000 for 6 recipients.

DEADLINE: Refer to the website for the next application cycle.

PROVIDER: Horatio Alger Association of Distinguished Americans

WEBSITE: http://application.horatioalger.org

New Hampshire Department of Education

ELIGIBLE APPLICANT: Seniors

OVERVIEW: The state government. Refer to the Scholarship page of the website for information on New Hampshire scholarships. This page includes the Hood Milk Sportsman Scholarship and a scholarship for forestry and related forestry science study. Refer to the Financial Aid page of the website for financial aid programs.

WEBSITE: http://education.nh.gov/recognition/other.htm

New Hampshire Charitable Foundation

ELIGIBLE APPLICANT: Seniors

OVERVIEW: This community foundation is the largest private source for scholarships and other student aid in the state. New Hampshire students can complete one online application to a be considered for most programs. Refer to the website for information.

WEBSITE: www.nhcf.org/scholarships

Horatio Alger State Scholarship

ELIGIBLE APPLICANT: Seniors

OTHER ELIGIBILITY: New Hampshire resident. Financial Need ($55,000 or less adjusted gross family income). 2.0 GPA. Overcome significant adversity. U.S. citizen who will attend an accredited not-for-profit college in the U.S. on a full-time basis.

OVERVIEW: This program provides financial aid to students who faced and overcame great obstacles. The application requires a detailed description and verification of the adversity. Students are also evaluated on their involvement in school and community service activities. Refer to the Scholarship Programs page of the website for additional information.

AWARD: $7,000 for 5 recipients.

DEADLINE: Refer to the website for the next application cycle.

PROVIDER: Horatio Alger Association of Distinguished Americans

WEBSITE: http://application.horatioalger.org

Stephen Phillips Memorial Scholarship Fund

ELIGIBLE APPLICANT: Seniors

OTHER ELIGIBILITY: New Hampshire resident. 3.0 GPA. Financial Need. U.S. citizen or permanent resident. Students who will attend an accredited four-year college in the U.S.

OVERVIEW: An annual memorial scholarship for New England students with financial need who display high academic, citizenship and character achievements. Refer to the website for a financial need eligibility calculator.

AWARD: $3,000 to $18,000 renewable annually. The number of awards varies, but approximately 140 awards were provided in 2015.

DEADLINE: April for early applications. May for general applications.

PROVIDER: The Stephen Phillips Memorial Scholarship Fund, Inc.

WEBSITE: www.phillips-scholarship.org/about-us/history-of-the-award

New Jersey Higher Education Student Assistance Authority

OVERVIEW: The state government. The state has a program called NJ STARS for attending a community college in New Jersey and NJ STARS II for attending a four-year college in New Jersey. Both programs offer scholarships that are based on financial need & merit. For NJ Stars II, the financial need eligibility is household income under $250,000. The state also has a Governor's Urban Scholarship, which is a merit-based scholarship for students in economically-challenged communities. There are additional scholarships for unique situations. Refer to the Grants & Scholarships page of the website.

WEBSITE: www.hesaa.org/Pages/NJGrantsApplications.aspx

Champion Scholars Scholarship

ELIGIBLE APPLICANT: Seniors

OTHER ELIGIBILITY: New Jersey resident. 3.0 GPA. Students who will attend an accredited two-year or four-year college.

OVERVIEW: An annual scholarship program for students in five states. Students are evaluated on academic achievement, awards, volunteerism and their response to the essay question "What makes you a champion in your school or in your community?"

AWARD: $5,000 for the winner. $3,000 for second place. $2,000 for third place.

DEADLINE: April

PROVIDER: Champion Energy Services

WEBSITE: www.championenergyservices.com/programs/scholarship

Horatio Alger State Scholarship

ELIGIBLE APPLICANT: Seniors

OTHER ELIGIBILITY: New Jersey resident. Financial Need ($55,000 or less adjusted gross family income). 2.0 GPA. Overcome significant adversity. U.S. citizen who will attend an accredited not-for-profit college in the U.S.

OVERVIEW: This program provides financial aid to students who faced and overcame great obstacles. The application requires a detailed description and verification of the adversity. Students are also evaluated on their involvement in school and community service activities. Refer to the Scholarship Programs page of the website for additional information.

AWARD: $7,000 for 14 recipients.

DEADLINE: Refer to the website for the next application cycle.

PROVIDER: Horatio Alger Association of Distinguished Americans

WEBSITE: http://application.horatioalger.org

Janet Logan Daily Foundation Scholarship

ELIGIBLE APPLICANT: Seniors

OTHER ELIGIBILITY: New Jersey resident. 2.5 GPA. Worked an average of 30 hours per week during the summer since age 16. Students who will attend an accredited college in the U.S.

OVERVIEW: A memorial scholarship. Students must be actively participating in at least one extra-curricular activity. Students complete all 8 sections of the online application and have the application verified by their guidance counselor. Financial need is not a qualifier, but may be considered.

AWARD: $2,500 renewable annually ($10,000 in total) for one recipient.

DEADLINE: April

PROVIDER: Janet Logan Daily Foundation

WEBSITE: www.janetlogandailyfoundation.org/application.asp

Monks Service Scholarship

ELIGIBLE APPLICANT: Seniors

OTHER ELIGIBILITY: New Jersey resident with a permanent address within Monk's 52 service area towns. U.S. citizen who will attend an accredited college in the Fall after high school graduation.

OVERVIEW: A scholarship for students who demonstrate a commitment to community service. Winners will be selected based on the content and quality of their essay. Special consideration will be given to students who have shown leadership or entrepreneurship with their community service activities. Refer to the website for Monk's service areas.

AWARD: $2,000. 5 awards are provided.

DEADLINE: April 20, 2016.

PROVIDER: Monk's Home Improvements

WEBSITE: http://monkshomeimprovements.com/scholarship

New Jersey School Counselor Association Scholarship

ELIGIBLE APPLICANT: Seniors

OTHER ELIGIBILITY: New Jersey resident attending high school in New Jersey. Students accepted by and enrolling in a college.

OVERVIEW: A scholarship to recognize the important role of school counselors. Students write an essay (300-500 words) describing how their school counselor influenced their lives in a positive way. The school counselor must be a current member of the New Jersey School Counselor Association.

AWARD: $1,000 to three recipients.

DEADLINE: March

PROVIDER: New Jersey School Counselor Association

WEBSITE: www.njsca.org/high-school-scholarship

New Jersey Schoolwomen's Club Scholarships

ELIGIBLE APPLICANT: Seniors

OTHER ELIGIBILITY: New Jersey resident attending high school in New Jersey. Women intending to pursue a career in education (minimum of baccalaureate).

OVERVIEW: A scholarship program to promote the education profession, encourage women to become educators, and recognizing outstanding women in the field of education. Applicants will be evaluated on academic achievement and involvement in extra-curriculum activities and community service.

AWARD: $1,000 to 3 recipients and $500 to 2 recipients.

DEADLINE: Typically in February.

PROVIDER: New Jersey Schoolwomen's Club

WEBSITE: www.njschoolwomens.org/scholarship.html

Portuguese-American Scholarship Foundation Scholarships

ELIGIBLE APPLICANT: Seniors

OTHER ELIGIBILITY: New Jersey residency for 12 consecutive months. U.S. citizen or permanent resident. Students born in Portugal or having a parent or grandparent that was born in Portugal. Financial Need. Students enrolling in a four-year college.

OVERVIEW: A scholarship program to assist New Jersey students of Portuguese ancestry who demonstrate financial to further their education.

AWARD: Up to $8,000. The number of awards varies.

DEADLINE: March. Refer to the website for the next deadline.

PROVIDER: Portuguese-American Scholarship Foundation

WEBSITE: www.vivaportugal.com/pasf

New Mexico Higher Education Department

OVERVIEW: The state government. Refer to the Students & Parents page of the website for information on New Mexico financial aid programs, scholarships, college planning tips and other resources.

WEBSITE: www.hed.state.nm.us

Horatio Alger State Scholarship

ELIGIBLE APPLICANT: Seniors

OTHER ELIGIBILITY: New Mexico resident. Financial Need ($55,000 or less adjusted gross family income). 2.0 GPA. Overcome significant adversity. U.S. citizen who will attend an accredited not-for-profit college in the U.S. on a full-time basis.

OVERVIEW: This program provides financial aid to students who faced and overcame great obstacles. The application requires a detailed description and verification of the adversity. Students are also evaluated on their involvement in school and community service activities. Refer to the Scholarship Programs page of the website for additional information.

AWARD: $7,000 for 5 recipients.

DEADLINE: Refer to the website for the next application cycle.

PROVIDER: Horatio Alger Association of Distinguished Americans

WEBSITE: http://application.horatioalger.org

New York State Higher Education Services Corporation

OVERVIEW: The state government. Refer to the website for information on New York financial aid programs, scholarships, college planning tips and other resources.

WEBSITE: www.hesc.ny.gov

Financial Service Centers of New York Scholarship

ELIGIBLE APPLICANT: Seniors

OTHER ELIGIBILITY: New York City five boroughs and surrounding counties residents. 50 hours of community service each school year.

OVERVIEW: FSCNY and MoneyGram International provide annual scholarships for high achieving students in the greater New York City area. Students are selected based on academic achievement and demonstrated leadership skills at school and in the community.

AWARD: Up to $7,500. The number of awards varies.

DEADLINE: March. Refer to the website for the next application cycle.

PROVIDER: Financial Service Centers of New York

WEBSITE: www.fscny.org/?controller=scholarshipprogram

Horatio Alger State Scholarship

ELIGIBLE APPLICANT: Seniors

OTHER ELIGIBILITY: New York resident. Financial Need ($55,000 or less adjusted gross family income). 2.0 GPA. Overcome significant adversity. U.S. citizen who will attend an accredited not-for-profit college in the U.S.

OVERVIEW: This program provides financial aid to students who faced and overcame great obstacles. The application requires a detailed description and verification of the adversity. Students are also evaluated on their involvement in school and community service activities. Refer to the Scholarship Programs page of the website for additional information.

AWARD: $7,000 for 25 recipients.

DEADLINE: Refer to the website for the next application cycle.

PROVIDER: Horatio Alger Association of Distinguished Americans

WEBSITE: http://application.horatioalger.org

The New York Times College Scholarship Program

ELIGIBLE APPLICANT: Seniors

OTHER ELIGIBILITY: New York City resident. Financial Need. Students in top 10% of class. U.S. citizen or permanent resident.

OVERVIEW: This program provides scholarships for high achieving students in the greater New York City area in need of financial aid. The program includes mentoring and a summer internship with the NY Times.

AWARD: Up to $7,500 renewable annually (up to $30,000 total) for 10 recipients.

DEADLINE: October. Refer to the website for the next application cycle.

PROVIDER: The New York Times

WEBSITE: www.nytco.com/social-responsibility/college-scholarship-program

North Carolina State Education Assistance Authority

OVERVIEW: The state government. Refer to the Paying for College page of the website for information on North Carolina financial aid programs, scholarships, college planning tips and other resources.

WEBSITE: www.ncseaa.edu

Horatio Alger State Scholarship

ELIGIBLE APPLICANT: Seniors

OTHER ELIGIBILITY: North Carolina resident. Financial Need ($55,000 or less adjusted gross family income). 2.0 GPA. Overcome significant adversity. U.S. citizen who will attend an accredited not-for-profit college in the U.S. on a full-time basis.

OVERVIEW: This program provides financial aid to students who faced and overcame great obstacles. The application requires a detailed description and verification of the adversity. Students are also evaluated on their involvement in school and community service activities. Refer to the Scholarship Programs page of the website for additional information.

AWARD: $7,000 for 13 recipients.

DEADLINE: Refer to the website for the next application cycle.

PROVIDER: Horatio Alger Association of Distinguished Americans

WEBSITE: http://application.horatioalger.org

North Dakota University System

OVERVIEW: The state government. Refer to the Colleges & Universities; Students; Paying for College page of the website for information on North Dakota financial aid programs, scholarships, student loans and other resources.

WEBSITE: www.ndus.edu

Horatio Alger State Scholarship

ELIGIBLE APPLICANT: Seniors

OTHER ELIGIBILITY: North Dakota resident. Financial Need ($55,000 or less adjusted gross family income). 2.0 GPA. Overcome significant adversity. U.S. citizen who will attend an accredited not-for-profit college in the U.S. on a full-time basis.

OVERVIEW: This program provides financial aid to students who faced and overcame great obstacles. The application requires a detailed description and verification of the adversity. Students are also evaluated on their involvement in school and community service activities. Refer to the Scholarship Programs page of the website for additional information.

AWARD: $7,000 for 28 recipients.

DEADLINE: Refer to the website for the next application cycle.

PROVIDER: Horatio Alger Association of Distinguished Americans

WEBSITE: http://application.horatioalger.org

Ohio Department of Higher Education

OVERVIEW: The state government. Refer to the Students page of the website for information on Ohio financial aid programs, scholarships, federal aid programs and other resources.

WEBSITE: www.ohiohighered.org

Champion Scholars Scholarship

ELIGIBLE APPLICANT: Seniors

OTHER ELIGIBILITY: Ohio resident. 3.0 GPA. Students who will attend an accredited two-year or four-year college.

OVERVIEW: An annual scholarship program for students in five states. Students are evaluated on academic achievement, awards, volunteerism and their response to the essay question “What makes you a champion in your school or in your community?”

AWARD: $5,000 for the winner. $3,000 for second place. $2,000 for third place.

DEADLINE: April

PROVIDER: Champion Energy Services

WEBSITE: www.championenergyservices.com/programs/scholarship

Horatio Alger State Scholarship

ELIGIBLE APPLICANT: Seniors

OTHER ELIGIBILITY: Ohio resident. Financial Need ($55,000 or less adjusted gross family income). 2.0 GPA. Overcome significant adversity. U.S. citizen who will attend an accredited not-for-profit college in the U.S.

OVERVIEW: This program provides financial aid to students who faced and overcame great obstacles. The application requires a detailed description and verification of the adversity. Students are also evaluated on their involvement in school and community service activities. Refer to the Scholarship Programs page of the website for additional information.

AWARD: $10,000 for 4 recipients.

DEADLINE: Refer to the website for the next application cycle.

PROVIDER: Horatio Alger Association of Distinguished Americans

WEBSITE: http://application.horatioalger.org

The Anthony Munoz Foundation Scholarships

ELIGIBLE APPLICANT: Seniors

OTHER ELIGIBILITY: Ohio residents in the greater Cincinnati area.

OVERVIEW: There are two scholarships programs. The Scholarship Fund is a financial need-based scholarship of $20,000 to specific colleges in Kentucky, Indiana and Ohio. It requires a 2.5 GPA or 18 ACT along with other criteria. The Straight A Scholarship is a merit-based scholarship of $2,000 to 18 recipients. It requires a 3.0 GPA and other criteria. Refer to the website for specific scholarship eligibility and application requirements and for the 22 eligible counties.

AWARD: The amount and number of awards varies by scholarship.

DEADLINE: Refer to the website for the specific scholarship deadline.

PROVIDER: The Anthony Munoz Foundation

WEBSITE: www.munozfoundation.org/default.asp?contentid=5

Oklahoma State Regents for Higher Education

OVERVIEW: The state government. Refer to the website for information on Oklahoma financial aid programs, scholarships, federal aid programs and other resources.

WEBSITE: www.okhighered.org

Horatio Alger State Scholarship

ELIGIBLE APPLICANT: Seniors

OTHER ELIGIBILITY: Oklahoma resident. Financial Need ($55,000 or less adjusted gross family income). 2.0 GPA. Overcome significant adversity. U.S. citizen who will attend an accredited not-for-profit college in the U.S. on a full-time basis.

OVERVIEW: This program provides financial aid to students who faced and overcame great obstacles. The application requires a detailed description and verification of the adversity. Students are also evaluated on their involvement in school and community service activities. Refer to the Scholarship Programs page of the website for additional information.

AWARD: $7,000 for 8 recipients.

DEADLINE: Refer to the website for the next application cycle.

PROVIDER: Horatio Alger Association of Distinguished Americans

WEBSITE: http://application.horatioalger.org

Oregon Office of Student Access and Completion

OVERVIEW: The state government. Refer to the Grants page and the Scholarship page of the website for information on Oregon financial aid programs and scholarships.

WEBSITE: www.oregonstudentaid.gov/scholarships.aspx

Horatio Alger State Scholarship

ELIGIBLE APPLICANT: Seniors

OTHER ELIGIBILITY: Oregon resident. Financial Need ($55,000 or less adjusted gross family income). 2.0 GPA. Overcome significant adversity. U.S. citizen who will attend an accredited not-for-profit college in the U.S. on a full-time basis.

OVERVIEW: This program provides financial aid to students who faced and overcame great obstacles. The application requires a detailed description and verification of the adversity. Students are also evaluated on their involvement in school and community service activities. Refer to the Scholarship Programs page of the website for additional information.

AWARD: $7,000 for 5 recipients.

DEADLINE: Refer to the website for the next application cycle.

PROVIDER: Horatio Alger Association of Distinguished Americans

WEBSITE: http://application.horatioalger.org

Pennsylvania Higher Education Assistance Agency

OVERVIEW: The state government. Refer to the website for information on Pennsylvania financial aid programs, scholarships, student loans and other resources.

WEBSITE: www.pheaa.org

Champion Scholars Scholarship

ELIGIBLE APPLICANT: Seniors

OTHER ELIGIBILITY: Pennsylvania resident. 3.0 GPA. Students who will attend an accredited two-year or four-year college.

OVERVIEW: An annual scholarship program for students in five states. Students are evaluated on academic achievement, awards, volunteerism and their response to the essay question "What makes you a champion in your school or in your community?"

AWARD: $5,000 for the winner. $3,000 for second place. $2,000 for third place.

DEADLINE: April

PROVIDER: Champion Energy Services

WEBSITE: www.championenergyservices.com/programs/scholarship

Horatio Alger State Scholarship

ELIGIBLE APPLICANT: Seniors

OTHER ELIGIBILITY: Pennsylvania resident. Financial Need ($55,000 or less adjusted gross family income). 2.0 GPA. Overcome significant adversity. U.S. citizen who will attend an accredited not-for-profit college in the U.S. on a full-time basis.

OVERVIEW: This program provides financial aid to students who faced and overcame great obstacles. The application requires a detailed description and verification of the adversity. Students are also evaluated on their involvement in school and community service activities. Refer to the Scholarship Programs page of the website for additional information.

AWARD: $7,000 for 55 recipients.

DEADLINE: Refer to the website for the next application cycle.

PROVIDER: Horatio Alger Association of Distinguished Americans

WEBSITE: http://application.horatioalger.org

Road to Safety Scholarship

ELIGIBLE APPLICANT: Seniors

OTHER ELIGIBILITY: Pennsylvania residents planning to attend college.

OVERVIEW: An annual scholarship contest about the dangers of teenage drunk and distracted driving. Students can submit any type of project including a video, poster, poem, painting, drawing, song, brochure and website. The projects are judged on theme, motivation and creativity.

AWARD: $1,000 to the winner. $750 for second place. $500 for third place.

DEADLINE: May. Refer to the website for the next deadline.

PROVIDER: Metzger Wickersham

WEBSITE: www.arrivealivepa.com

Rhode Island Higher Education Assistance Authority

OVERVIEW: The state government. Refer to the website for information on Rhode Island financial aid programs, scholarships, student loans and other resources.

WEBSITE: www.riheaa.org

Horatio Alger State Scholarship

ELIGIBLE APPLICANT: Seniors

OTHER ELIGIBILITY: Rhode Island resident. Financial Need ($55,000 or less adjusted gross family income). 2.0 GPA. Overcome significant adversity. U.S. citizen who will attend an accredited not-for-profit college in the U.S. on a full-time basis.

OVERVIEW: This program provides financial aid to students who faced and overcame great obstacles. The application requires a detailed description and verification of the adversity. Students are also evaluated on their involvement in school and community service activities. Refer to the Scholarship Programs page of the website for additional information.

AWARD: $7,000 for 5 recipients.

DEADLINE: Refer to the website for the next application cycle.

PROVIDER: Horatio Alger Association of Distinguished Americans

WEBSITE: http://application.horatioalger.org

Shaw-Worth Memorial Scholarship

ELIGIBLE APPLICANT: Seniors

OTHER ELIGIBILITY: Connecticut resident.

OVERVIEW: This program rewards New England students who work with and on behalf of animals. Examples include leadership in animal protection organizations and rescue of animals in danger. Applicants write a letter which includes a description of their achievements in animal protection, attitude toward animals, a description of their activities to promote animal protection and their plans for future animal protection work.

AWARD: up to $3,500. The number of awards varies.

DEADLINE: March. Refer to the website for the next application cycle.

PROVIDER: The Humane Society of the United States

WEBSITE: www.humanesociety.org/parents_educators/teens/shaw_worth_scholarship.html

Stephen Phillips Memorial Scholarship Fund

ELIGIBLE APPLICANT: Seniors

OTHER ELIGIBILITY: Rhode Island resident. 3.0 GPA. Financial Need. U.S. citizen or permanent resident. Students who will attend an accredited four-year college in the U.S.

OVERVIEW: An annual memorial scholarship for New England students with financial need who display high academic, citizenship and character achievements. Refer to the website for a financial need eligibility calculator.

AWARD: $3,000 to $18,000 renewable annually. The number of awards varies, but approximately 140 awards were provided in 2015.

DEADLINE: April for early applications. May for general applications.

PROVIDER: The Stephen Phillips Memorial Scholarship Fund, Inc.

WEBSITE: www.phillips-scholarship.org/about-us/history-of-the-award

South Carolina Commission on Higher Education

OVERVIEW: The state government. Refer to the Students, Families & Military page of the website for information on South Carolina financial aid programs, scholarships, college planning tips and other resources.

WEBSITE: www.che.sc.gov

Horatio Alger State Scholarship

ELIGIBLE APPLICANT: Seniors

OTHER ELIGIBILITY: South Carolina resident. Financial Need ($55,000 or less adjusted gross family income). 2.0 GPA. Overcome significant adversity. U.S. citizen who will attend an accredited not-for-profit college in the U.S. on a full-time basis.

OVERVIEW: This program provides financial aid to students who faced and overcame great obstacles. The application requires a detailed description and verification of the adversity. Students are also evaluated on their involvement in school and community service activities. Refer to the Scholarship Programs page of the website for additional information.

AWARD: $7,000 for 6 recipients.

DEADLINE: Refer to the website for the next application cycle.

PROVIDER: Horatio Alger Association of Distinguished Americans

WEBSITE: http://application.horatioalger.org

South Dakota Department of Education

OVERVIEW: The state government. Refer to the Scholarships page of the website for information on South Dakota scholarships.

WEBSITE: www.doe.sd.gov/secretary/scholarships.aspx

Horatio Alger State Scholarship

ELIGIBLE APPLICANT: Seniors

OTHER ELIGIBILITY: South Dakota resident. Financial Need ($55,000 or less adjusted gross family income). 2.0 GPA. Overcome significant adversity. U.S. citizen who will attend an accredited not-for-profit college in the U.S. on a full-time basis.

OVERVIEW: This program provides financial aid to students who faced and overcame great obstacles. The application requires a detailed description and verification of the adversity. Students are also evaluated on their involvement in school and community service activities. Refer to the Scholarship Programs page of the website for additional information.

AWARD: $7,000 for 32 recipients.

DEADLINE: Refer to the website for the next application cycle.

PROVIDER: Horatio Alger Association of Distinguished Americans

WEBSITE: http://application.horatioalger.org

Tennessee Student Assistance Corporation

OVERVIEW: The state government. Refer to the Students page of the website for information on Tennessee financial aid programs, scholarships, federal aid programs and other resources.

WEBSITE: http://tn.gov/collegepays/section/money-for-college

Horatio Alger State Scholarship

ELIGIBLE APPLICANT: Seniors

OTHER ELIGIBILITY: Tennessee resident. Financial Need ($55,000 or less adjusted gross family income). 2.0 GPA. Overcome significant adversity. U.S. citizen who will attend an accredited not-for-profit college in the U.S. on a full-time basis.

OVERVIEW: This program provides financial aid to students who faced and overcame great obstacles. The application requires a detailed description and verification of the adversity. Students are also evaluated on their involvement in school and community service activities. Refer to the Scholarship Programs page of the website for additional information.

AWARD: $7,000 for 9 recipients.

DEADLINE: Refer to the website for the next application cycle.

PROVIDER: Horatio Alger Association of Distinguished Americans

WEBSITE: http://application.horatioalger.org

Texas Higher Education Coordinating Board

OVERVIEW: The state government. Refer to the website for information on Texas financial aid programs, scholarships, federal aid programs and other resources.

WEBSITE: www.hhloans.com/apps/financialaid/tofa.cfm?Kind=GS

Champion Scholars Scholarship

ELIGIBLE APPLICANT: Seniors

OTHER ELIGIBILITY: Texas resident. 3.0 GPA. Students who will attend an accredited two-year or four-year college.

OVERVIEW: An annual scholarship program for students in five states. Students are evaluated on academic achievement, awards, volunteerism and their response to the essay question "What makes you a champion in your school or in your community?"

AWARD: $5,000 for the winner. $3,000 for second place. $2,000 for third place.

DEADLINE: April

PROVIDER: Champion Energy Services

WEBSITE: www.championenergyservices.com/programs/scholarship

Horatio Alger State Scholarship

ELIGIBLE APPLICANT: Seniors

OTHER ELIGIBILITY: Texas resident. Financial Need ($55,000 or less adjusted gross family income). 2.0 GPA. Overcome significant adversity. U.S. citizen who will attend an accredited not-for-profit college in the U.S. on a full-time basis.

OVERVIEW: This program provides financial aid to students who faced and overcame great obstacles. The application requires a detailed description and verification of the adversity. Students are also evaluated on their involvement in school and community service activities. Refer to the Scholarship Programs page of the website for additional information.

AWARD: $7,000 for 25 recipients.

DEADLINE: Refer to the website for the next application cycle.

PROVIDER: Horatio Alger Association of Distinguished Americans

WEBSITE: http://application.horatioalger.org

Utah Higher Education Assistance Authority

OVERVIEW: The state government. Refer to the website for information on Utah financial aid programs, scholarships, federal aid programs and other resources.

WEBSITE: www.uheaa.org

Horatio Alger State Scholarship

ELIGIBLE APPLICANT: Seniors

OTHER ELIGIBILITY: Utah resident. Financial Need ($55,000 or less adjusted gross family income). 2.0 GPA. Overcome significant adversity. U.S. citizen who will attend an accredited not-for-profit college in the U.S. on a full-time basis.

OVERVIEW: This program provides financial aid to students who faced and overcame great obstacles. The application requires a detailed description and verification of the adversity. Students are also evaluated on their involvement in school and community service activities. Refer to the Scholarship Programs page of the website for additional information.

AWARD: $7,000 for 7 recipients.

DEADLINE: Refer to the website for the next application cycle.

PROVIDER: Horatio Alger Association of Distinguished Americans

WEBSITE: http://application.horatioalger.org

Vermont Student Assistance Corporation

OVERVIEW: The state government. Refer to the website for information on Vermont financial aid programs, scholarships, federal aid programs and other resources.

WEBSITE: http://services.vsac.org/wps/wcm/connect/vsac/VSAC

Horatio Alger State Scholarship

ELIGIBLE APPLICANT: Seniors

OTHER ELIGIBILITY: Vermont resident. Financial Need ($55,000 or less adjusted gross family income). 2.0 GPA. Overcome significant adversity. U.S. citizen who will attend an accredited not-for-profit college in the U.S. on a full-time basis.

OVERVIEW: This program provides financial aid to students who faced and overcame great obstacles. The application requires a detailed description and verification of the adversity. Students are also evaluated on their involvement in school and community service activities. Refer to the Scholarship Programs page of the website for additional information.

AWARD: $7,000 for 5 recipients.

DEADLINE: Refer to the website for the next application cycle.

PROVIDER: Horatio Alger Association of Distinguished Americans

WEBSITE: http://application.horatioalger.org

Shaw-Worth Memorial Scholarship

ELIGIBLE APPLICANT: Seniors

OTHER ELIGIBILITY: Connecticut resident.

OVERVIEW: This program rewards New England students who work with and on behalf of animals. Examples include leadership in animal protection organizations and rescue of animals in danger. Applicants write a letter which includes a description of their achievements in animal protection, attitude toward animals, a description of their activities to promote animal protection and their plans for future animal protection work.

AWARD: up to $3,500. The number of awards varies.

DEADLINE: March. Refer to the website for the next application cycle.

PROVIDER: The Humane Society of the United States

WEBSITE: www.humanesociety.org/parents_educators/teens/shaw_worth_scholarship.html

Stephen Phillips Memorial Scholarship Fund

ELIGIBLE APPLICANT: Seniors

OTHER ELIGIBILITY: Vermont resident. 3.0 GPA. Financial Need. U.S. citizen or permanent resident. Students who will attend an accredited four-year college in the U.S.

OVERVIEW: An annual memorial scholarship for New England students with financial need who display high academic, citizenship and character achievements. Refer to the website for a financial need eligibility calculator.

AWARD: $3,000 to $18,000 renewable annually. The number of awards varies, but approximately 140 awards were provided in 2015.

DEADLINE: April for early applications. May for general applications.

PROVIDER: The Stephen Phillips Memorial Scholarship Fund, Inc.

WEBSITE: www.phillips-scholarship.org/about-us/history-of-the-award

State Council of Higher Education for Virginia

OVERVIEW: The state government. Refer to the website for information on Virginia financial aid programs, scholarships, and other resources.

WEBSITE: www.schev.edu/students/undergradFinancialaid Programs.asp

Horatio Alger State Scholarship

ELIGIBLE APPLICANT: Seniors

OTHER ELIGIBILITY: Virginia resident. Financial Need ($55,000 or less adjusted gross family income). 2.0 GPA. Overcome significant adversity. U.S. citizen who will attend an accredited not-for-profit college in the U.S. on a full-time basis.

OVERVIEW: This program provides financial aid to students who faced and overcame great obstacles. The application requires a detailed description and verification of the adversity. Students are also evaluated on their involvement in school and community service activities. Refer to the Scholarship Programs page of the website for additional information.

AWARD: $7,000. The number of awards varies.

DEADLINE: Refer to the website for the next application cycle.

PROVIDER: Horatio Alger Association of Distinguished Americans

WEBSITE: http://application.horatioalger.org

Washington Student Achievement Council

OVERVIEW: The state government. Refer to the Financial Aid page of the website for information on Washington financial aid programs, scholarships, and other resources.

WEBSITE: www.wsac.wa.gov/sfa-overview

Horatio Alger State Scholarship

ELIGIBLE APPLICANT: Seniors

OTHER ELIGIBILITY: Washington resident. Financial Need ($55,000 or less adjusted gross family income). 2.0 GPA. Overcome significant adversity. U.S. citizen who will attend an accredited not-for-profit college in the U.S.

OVERVIEW: This program provides financial aid to students who faced and overcame great obstacles. The application requires a detailed description and verification of the adversity. Students are also evaluated on their involvement in school and community service activities. Refer to the Scholarship Programs page of the website for additional information.

AWARD: $7,000 for 10 recipients.

DEADLINE: Refer to the website for the next application cycle.

PROVIDER: Horatio Alger Association of Distinguished Americans

WEBSITE: http://application.horatioalger.org

Washington Scholarship Coalition

OVERVIEW: A scholarship search website that connects Washington students with Washington scholarship providers.

WEBSITE: www.thewashboard.org/login.aspx

West Virginia Higher Education Policy Commission

OVERVIEW: The state government. Refer to the Resources; Financial Aid page of the website for information on West Virginia financial aid programs, scholarships and other resources.

WEBSITE: www.wvhepc.com

Horatio Alger State Scholarship

ELIGIBLE APPLICANT: Seniors

OTHER ELIGIBILITY: West Virginia resident. Financial Need ($55,000 or less adjusted gross family income). 2.0 GPA. Overcome significant adversity. U.S. citizen who will attend an accredited not-for-profit college in the U.S. on a full-time basis.

OVERVIEW: This program provides financial aid to students who faced and overcame great obstacles. The application requires a detailed description and verification of the adversity. Students are also evaluated on their involvement in school and community service activities. Refer to the Scholarship Programs page of the website for additional information.

AWARD: $7,000 for 6 recipients.

DEADLINE: Refer to the website for the next application cycle.

PROVIDER: Horatio Alger Association of Distinguished Americans

WEBSITE: http://application.horatioalger.org

State of Wisconsin Higher Educational Aids Board

OVERVIEW: The state government. Refer to the website for information on Wisconsin financial aid programs, grants, scholarships, student loans and other resources.

WEBSITE: www.heab.state.wi.us

Horatio Alger State Scholarship

ELIGIBLE APPLICANT: Seniors

OTHER ELIGIBILITY: Wisconsin resident. Financial Need ($55,000 or less adjusted gross family income). 2.0 GPA. Overcome significant adversity. U.S. citizen who will attend an accredited not-for-profit college in the U.S. on a full-time basis.

OVERVIEW: This program provides financial aid to students who faced and overcame great obstacles. The application requires a detailed description and verification of the adversity. Students are also evaluated on their involvement in school and community service activities. Refer to the Scholarship Programs page of the website for additional information.

AWARD: $7,000 for 10 recipients.

DEADLINE: Refer to the website for the next application cycle.

PROVIDER: Horatio Alger Association of Distinguished Americans

WEBSITE: http://application.horatioalger.org

Wyoming Department of Education

OVERVIEW: The state government. Refer to the website for information on Wyoming financial aid programs, scholarships and other resources.

WEBSITE: www.edu.wyoming.gov

Horatio Alger State Scholarship

ELIGIBLE APPLICANT: Seniors

OTHER ELIGIBILITY: Wyoming resident. Financial Need ($55,000 or less adjusted gross family income). 2.0 GPA. Overcome significant adversity. U.S. citizen who will attend an accredited not-for-profit college in the U.S. on a full-time basis.

OVERVIEW: This program provides financial aid to students who faced and overcame great obstacles. The application requires a detailed description and verification of the adversity. Students are also evaluated on their involvement in school and community service activities. Refer to the Scholarship Programs page of the website for additional information.

AWARD: $7,000 for 5 recipients.

DEADLINE: Refer to the website for the next application cycle.

PROVIDER: Horatio Alger Association of Distinguished Americans

WEBSITE: http://application.horatioalger.org

Chapter Nine

Other Options for Scholarships

Scholarships Provided Directly by Colleges

Most colleges award merit-based and financial need-based scholarships directly to students as part of an admissions package. These scholarships come from the college or a department within the college. Students may not need to apply separately for these scholarships. At many colleges, students are automatically considered for scholarships when they apply for admission. However, for the more prestigious scholarships, students will likely need to provide additional information or attend an interview. In addition, some of the colleges require students to apply for admission early to be considered for a scholarship. For these colleges, the "general" admission deadline is too late for scholarship consideration. Students should review the website of every college that they are considering applying to for information on available scholarships, deadlines and whether a separate application is required. Students should also contact the college financial aid office for information.

Scholarships Provided for Specific Colleges by Alumni & Others

Scholarships to specific colleges are often available from individuals and organizations that are affiliated or have a partnership with those colleges or are located in the same community. In addition, scholarships are often available from alumni. Students will typically need to apply directly for these scholarships. For example, a local business may be give back to the community by offering a scholarship to the local college. A corporation may sponsor a joint research grant with a college. Alumni may sponsor a scholarship for their college as a way to give back to their college. Depending on the alumni, the scholarship may have a degree or special interest requirement that the alumni associates with.

High School Counselor as a Source for Scholarships

High School Counselors/Guidance Counselors are a wealth of information on all aspects of the college application and admission process including college scholarships. In particular, school counselors have information on local scholarships that are not found in traditional search websites and books. This may include scholarships that are offered by high school organizations, such as thc Parent-Teacher Organization (PTO), high school clubs, such as the Honor Society and the Athletics Booster Club, high school memorial scholarships, scholarships provided by high school alumni to support students from their high school, and scholarships offered by local businesses, civic organizations and the community.

High School Websites as a Source for Scholarships

High school websites are often a good source of information for college scholarships. Students and parents may need to dig a few layers to locate them. They should not automatically assume that scholarships are not listed by only viewing the home page. In addition to the student's high school, students and parents should review websites from other high schools in their state. The other high school websites may contain local, county and state scholarships that students and parents were not aware of.

Scholarships for Employees

Some businesses and corporations offer college scholarships to their employees who are high school students. McDonalds and some of the larger retail chains are examples. High school students who are working part-time or full-time should inquire about college scholarships with their employer.

Scholarships for Children of Employees

Many businesses and corporations provide college scholarships to children of their employees. These scholarships are not typically advertised outside the company. Parents should contact their employer or employer's human resources department to inquire about scholarship opportunities for their children and the eligibility and application requirements.

Scholarships for Children and Grandchildren of Members of the Military

There are many college scholarships for children of members of the U.S. military. This applies to children of former military members and those currently servicing. This may also apply to grandchildren of former military members and those currently surviving. The scholarships may be intended for a specific U.S. military armed service branch or for any branch. Some of the scholarships are intended for children and grandchildren of veterans or those who are disabled or deceased due to their military service.

Each branch of the U.S. military provides college scholarships which typically extends to the children and possibly grandchildren of former members and those currently serving.

State governments are another source for college scholarships. Most if not all states fund college scholarships for children and sometimes grandchildren of current and former members of the military including veterans and those who are disabled or deceased due to their military service. Students should contact the Department of Higher Education and the Office of Veterans Affairs of their state government for information on available scholarships and the eligibility and application requirements.

Military non-profit foundations have been established to provide these college scholarships and to fundraise for future scholarships. For example, the Navy League Foundation at (www.navyleague.org) currently awards $2,500 renewable scholarships to twenty-five high school seniors. The Army Scholarship Foundation at (www.armyscholarshipfoundation.org) awards $500 to $2,000 renewable scholarships.

Memorial scholarships have been created to support current and former U.S. military personnel and their families.

Many organizations and corporations provide college scholarships to thank members of the military for service to their country and to provide educational support to their families. This includes veteran organizations, such as the Veterans of Foreign Wars (VFW) and the American Legion.

There are many ways to locate military-based scholarships, such as the internet, search websites, books and contacting the U.S. military armed service branches, government and organizations. Another option may be the website (www.military.com) which advertises 10 million members. This website has a military-specific college scholarship search finder.

Scholarships from Places of Worship

Students and parents should inquire about the availability of college scholarships with their place of worship. If their place of worship does not provide scholarships, they may have knowledge of scholarships offered by an affiliate or other organization of that faith.

Scholarships for Participation in Youth Recreational and Competitive Sports

Many youth and amateur sport leagues and organizations offer college scholarships to high school students who participated in that league or organization as individuals or on a team during their youth. This includes participation at a recreational level, working as a referee or umpire or volunteering for that league or organization.

Town and local recreational and travel sports leagues may offer college scholarships to former participants, employees and volunteers of that league. In addition, most town and local recreational and travel leagues are members of a national youth amateur sports organization for educational support and other resources and benefits. These national youth amateur sports organizations may provide college scholarships for high school students who participated in a member recreational or travel league while in their youth.

For students who participated in sports on a more competitive level, they were likely registered with many national youth amateur sports organizations by their coach or parents in order to participate in tournaments and competitions hosted or sponsored by those organizations. This would typically make the students eligible for college scholarships that are offered by those organizations.

The types of college scholarships offered by town, local and national youth amateur sport leagues and organizations vary from merit-based to financial need-based and are often not intended for athletic success. Some of the scholarships are intended to acknowledge former and current participants for their academic achievement, community service or service to that league or organization.

Students should compile a list of all sports that they participated in on a recreational, travel and competitive basis and in a paid or volunteer capacity and contact those leagues and organizations for scholarship availability.

Examples of national youth amateur sports organizations are:

- Amateur Athletic Union (AAU)
- American Legion Baseball
- Amateur Softball Association (ASA)
- American Youth Soccer Organization (AYSO)
- Babe Ruth Baseball & Softball
- Boys & Girls Clubs of America
- Dizzy Dean Baseball & Softball
- Dixie Youth Baseball & Softball
- Little League Baseball & Softball
- National American Sport Taekwondo Association (NASTA)
- National Field Archery Association
- Pony Baseball & Softball
- Pop Warner
- USA Field Hockey
- USA Gymnastics
- USA Hockey
- USA Swimming
- USA Volleyball
- USA Wrestling
- United States Basketball Association (USBA)
- United States Bowling Congress (USBC)
- U.S. Figure Skating
- U.S. Lacrosse
- U.S. Youth Soccer
- United States Specialty Sports Association (USSSA)

Scholarships from Local Civic & Social Clubs & Organizations

Local civic and social clubs and organizations represent another source for college scholarships. These scholarships may be intended for members, children of members or students from the community. Students should compile a list of all local civic and social clubs and organizations and contact them about the availability of scholarships. Examples are Boys & Girls Club of America, Boy Scouts, Elks, Girl Scouts, JCC, Kiwanis, Knights of Columbus, Lions Club, Rotary Club and YMCA. Students can review their local town or municipality website for a listing of civic and social groups.

Scholarship Search Websites

Students and parents that are interested in searching for college scholarships beyond the scholarships and search options identified in this book can use college scholarship search websites. There are many search websites to choose from. No two websites are alike nor do they list the identical scholarships. Some are free to use and others require a fee. Some have a "create a profile" feature that is intended to help narrow the search. A few websites advertise that they will send notifications to users when new scholarships are posted that match their profile. Some will be more accurate and current than others. Regardless of the search website, users must be willing to put in the time to read through the scholarship descriptions and determine for themselves whether they are eligible.

Examples of college scholarship search websites are:

- Adventures In Education at (*www.aie.org/scholarships)*
- Cappex at (*www.cappex.com/scholarships*)
- Chegg at (*www.chegg.com/scholarships*)
- CollegeBoard at (*www.collegeboard.org*)
- CollegeXpress at (*www.collegexpress.com/scholarships/search*)
- Common Knowledge Scholarship Foundation at (*www.cksf.org*)
- Fastweb at (*www.fastweb.com*)
- FinAid at (*www.finaid.org*)
- MoolahSpot at (*www.moolahspot.com*)
- NextStepU at (*www.nextstepu.com*)
- Nitche at (*www.colleges.niche.com/scholarships*)
- Peterson's at (*www.petersons.com*)
- SallieMae at (*www.salliemae.com)*
- Scholarship Monkey at (*www.scholarshipmonkey.com)*
- ScholarshipMentor at (*www.scholarshipmentor.com*)
- Scholarship America at (*www.scholarshipamerica.org*)
- Scholarship Detective at (*www.scholarshipdetective.com*)
- ScholarshipOnline at (*www.scholarshipsonline.org*)
- Scholarships.com at (*www.scholarships.com*)
- Scholarshippoints.com at (*www.scholarshippoints.com*)
- Scholly at (*www.myscholly.com*)
- StudentAdvisor at (*www.studentadvisor.com/scholarships/lists*)
- StudentScholarships at (*www.studentscholarships.org*)
- SuperCollege at (*www.supercollege.com*)
- Unigo at (*www.unigo.com/scholarships*)
- USAScholarships at (*www.usascholarships.com*)

The use of search websites will often be a time consuming and frustrating process. However, all of the search websites have value. Users should be able to locate additional scholarships that high school students are eligible for, especially the "specialty" and "state residency" scholarships.

Other Options for College Scholarships

Other options for locating or obtaining college scholarships include local and county libraries, town and county governments, minor league and professional sports teams, fraternities and sororities that parents belong to, charities and service organizations that students volunteered for, scholarships specifically for students with physical disabilities, local businesses, local stores that are part of large retail chains, professional organizations and unions that parents belong to, and local societies.

Chapter Ten

Final Thoughts

Now that you finished reading this book, you should be well on your way to locating many college scholarships that you are eligible to apply for. While the number and type of scholarships that you apply for is a personal choice, consider these finals thoughts.

Most scholarships receive many applicants. Depending on the amount of time that you can dedicate to the application process, you may decide to narrow your choices to scholarships that not only interest you, but give you the best odds at winning.

Local scholarships do not typically have as many applicants as national scholarships. In some cases, local scholarships receive very few applicants because students are not aware of them. However, local scholarships do not typically provide the large awards that you may receive with national scholarships.

Do not get discouraged if you do not receive a scholarship. There is a lot of competition and you can reapply for some of the scholarships in the following year. In addition, there are even more scholarship opportunities for students that are already enrolled in college.

Lastly, if you have a few minutes, please consider writing a review about the book. Good luck!

Index

Made in the USA
Middletown, DE
25 May 2016